**Fourth Grade**

# Everyday Mathematics®

## Assessment Handbook

## Fourth Grade

# Everyday Mathematics®

## Assessment Handbook

**The University of Chicago
School Mathematics Project**

Columbus, OH • Chicago, IL • Redmond, WA

The **McGraw·Hill** Companies

## UCSMP Elementary Materials Component
Max Bell, Director

**Authors**
Jean Bell
William M. Carroll

**Photo Credits**
Phil Martin/Photography
Cover: Bill Burlingham/Photography
Photo Collage: Herman Adler Design Group

**Acknowledgments**
We gratefully acknowledge the work of the following classroom
teachers who provided input and suggestions as we designed
this handbook:  Huong Bahn, Fran Moore, Jenny Waters,
and Lana Winnet.

**Contributors**
Ellen Dairyko, Amy Dillard, Sharon Draznin,
Nancy Hanvey, Laurie Leff, Denise Porter,
Herb Price, Joyce timmons, Lisa Winters

## www.sra4kids.com

Send all inquiries to:
SRA/McGraw-Hill
P.O. Box 812960
Chicago, IL 60681

Printed in the United States of America.

ISBN  0-07-600018-4

7 8 9 10 POH 08 07 06 05

The McGraw·Hill Companies

# Contents

# Introduction

Too often, school assessment is equated with testing and grading. While some formal assessment is necessary, it tends to provide only scattered snapshots of students rather than records of their growth and progress. The philosophy of *Everyday Mathematics*® is that real assessment should be more like a motion picture, revealing the development of the student's mathematical understanding while giving the teacher useful feedback about instructional needs. Rather than simply providing tests on isolated skills, *Everyday Mathematics* offers a variety of useful techniques and opportunities to assess students' progress on skills, concepts, and thinking processes.

Several assessment tools are built into the *Everyday Mathematics* program. Slate assessments and end-of-unit written assessments are useful in showing how well students are learning the concepts and skills covered in a unit. But these tools by themselves do not provide a balance, highlight progress, or show students' work on larger problems. The purpose of this handbook is to broaden your assessment techniques. Rather than using all of the techniques suggested here, choose a few that balance written work with observation, individual work with group work, and short answers with longer explanations.

For assessment to be valid and useful to both teachers and students, the authors believe that

- teachers need to have a variety of assessment tools and techniques from which to choose.

- students should be included in the assessment process through interviews, written work, and conferences that provide appropriate feedback. Self-assessment and reflection are skills that will develop over time if encouraged.

- assessment and instruction should be closely linked. Assessment should assist teachers in making instructional decisions concerning both individual students and the whole class.

- a good assessment plan makes instruction easier.

- the best assessment plans are those developed by teachers working collaboratively within their schools.

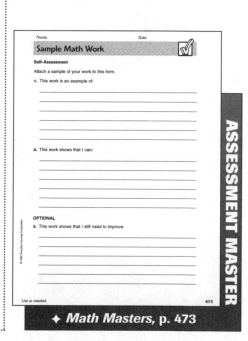

This handbook compiles classroom-tested techniques used by experienced *Everyday Mathematics* teachers. It includes suggestions for observing students, keeping anecdotal records, following student progress, and encouraging students to reflect on and communicate both what they have learned and how they feel about mathematics. Many of the assessment suggestions are aimed specifically at *Everyday Mathematics* activities, such as using partner activities and games to observe students and using Math Boxes to focus on a particular concept or skill.

As you read through this handbook, you may want to start with one or two activities that fit your needs and assist you in building a balanced approach to assessment. Feel free to adapt the materials to your own needs. While some teachers find Math Logs useful, others find observations and short, informal interviews more helpful.

The *Everyday Mathematics* goal is to furnish you with some ideas to make assessment and instruction more manageable, productive, and exciting; as well as offer you a more complete picture of each student's progress and instructional needs.

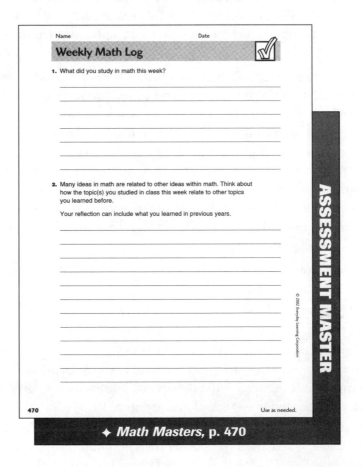

♦ *Math Masters, p. 470*

# A Balance of Assessments

## Ongoing, Product, and Periodic Assessments, and Outside Tests

Although there is no one "right" assessment plan for all classrooms, all assessment plans should use a variety of techniques. To develop your own plan, consider four different assessment sources within the Quad shown in the figure below.

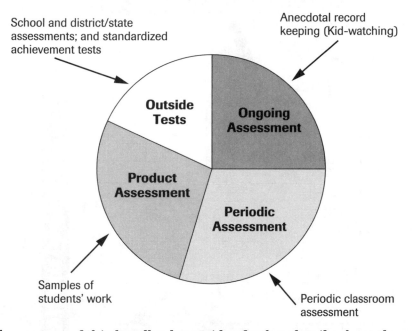

School and district/state assessments; and standardized achievement tests

Anecdotal record keeping (Kid-watching)

Outside Tests

Ongoing Assessment

Product Assessment

Periodic Assessment

Samples of students' work

Periodic classroom assessment

The content of this handbook provides further details about the assessment sources shown in the circle graph. Your own assessment plan should answer these questions:

• *How is the class doing as a whole?*
• *How are individual students doing?*
• *How do I need to adjust instructions to meet students' needs?*
• *How can I communicate to students, parents, and others about the progress being made?*

The proportions of assessment sources shown in the circle graph on page 3 are quite flexible and depend on a number of factors, such as experience of the students and time of year. At the beginning of the year, teachers might use a higher proportion of Ongoing and Product Assessment sources with smaller proportions of Periodic and Outside Test sources.

The section beginning on page 37 provides for each unit examples of how to use different types of assessments in specific lessons.

***Ongoing Assessment*** includes observations of student involvement in regular classroom activities, such as working with partners or small groups during games and working individually on Math Boxes. It may also include observations of students' thinking and shared strategies and information you gather from classroom interactions or from informal individual interviews. Records of these ongoing assessments may take the form of short, written notes; more elaborate record pages; or brief mental notes to yourself. See Ongoing Assessment, pages 15 and 16, for details.

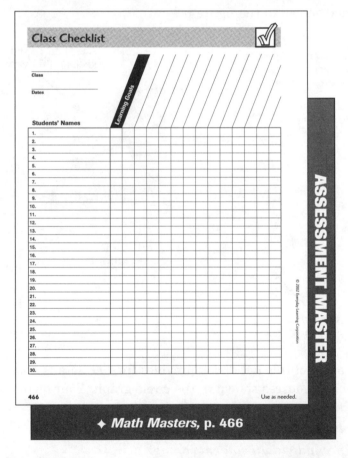

✦ *Math Masters, p. 466*

***Product Assessment*** may include samples of Math Boxes, journal pages, Study Links, solutions to open-ended problems, group project reports, mathematical writing, drawings, sketches, diagrams, and anything else you feel has value and reflects what you want learners to do. If you are keeping portfolios, students should help select which products to include. See Portfolios, pages 7–11, and Product Assessment, pages 17–22.

*Periodic Assessment* includes more formal assessments, such as end-of-unit assessments, cumulative reviews, quizzes, Class Progress Indicators, and math interest inventories. Pages 23–29 offer suggestions and extensions intended to help you measure both individual and class progress using these types of assessment.

*Outside Tests* provide information from school, district, state, and standardized tests that might be used to evaluate the progress of a student, class, or school. See page 33 for more information.

A List of Assessment Sources attached to students' folders or portfolios or kept in your record book may help you see whether you have included information from the first three sources of the Quad as well as from other sources. Notice that the completed sample shown below includes only a few of the assessment suggestions from each source. Another teacher might choose other entries. Using multiple techniques will give you a clear picture of each student's progress and instructional needs.

Use this List of Assessment Sources master to keep track of the assessment sources that you are currently using. A blank sample is provided as Math Masters, page 464, and is shown in reduced form on page 115 of this book.

NOTE: Do not try to use all assessment sources at once. Instead, devise a manageable, balanced plan.

Your assessment plan should answer these questions:

- *How is the class performing as a whole?*
- *How are individual students performing?*
- *How can I adjust instruction to meet students' needs?*
- *How can I communicate to students, parents, and others about the progress being made?*

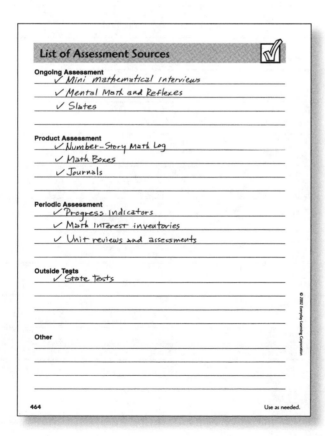

**List of Assessment Sources**

**Ongoing Assessment**
✓ Mini mathematical Interviews
✓ Mental Math and Reflexes
✓ Slates

**Product Assessment**
✓ Number-Story Math Log
✓ Math Boxes
✓ Journals

**Periodic Assessment**
✓ Progress Indicators
✓ Math Interest inventories
✓ Unit reviews and assessments

**Outside Tests**
✓ State Tests

**Other**

464                                    Use as needed.

## Your Assessment Ideas

_____
_____
_____
_____
_____
_____
_____
_____
_____
_____
_____
_____
_____
_____
_____
_____
_____
_____
_____
_____
_____
_____
_____
_____
_____
_____
_____

**Your Assessment Ideas**

# Portfolios

## Using Portfolios

Portfolios are used for a number of different purposes, from keeping track of progress to helping students become more reflective about their mathematical growth. The practice of keeping portfolios is a positive assessment technique and is consistent with the philosophy of *Everyday Mathematics* for the following reasons:

• Portfolios emphasize progress over time, rather than results at a given moment. At any time, a student may have Beginning, Developing, or Secure understandings of various mathematical concepts. This progress can best be exhibited by a collection of products organized into portfolios or folders that contain work from different contexts and from different times in the year.

• Portfolios can involve students more directly in the assessment process. Students may write introductions and help select portfolio entries. They can select work they are especially proud of and tag each piece with an explanation of why it was chosen. Developing realistic self-assessment is a valuable skill that takes time to acquire.

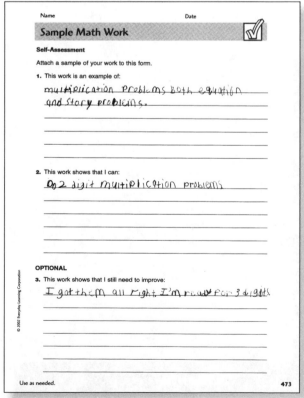

• Portfolios can be used as evidence of progress for students, their families, and their teachers for next year. You may want to establish a "Portfolio Night" for students and their parents to attend in order to allow them time to discuss and review portfolio contents. It is very important that parents understand the goals of the various projects and assignments.

• Portfolios can illustrate students' strengths and weaknesses in particular areas of mathematics. Since a rich body of work can be contained in a portfolio, it is a good vehicle for exhibiting each student's progress. Portfolios also can be used to assess students' abilities to see connections within mathematics and to apply mathematical ideas to real-world situations.

Some teachers keep two types of portfolios: a working portfolio in which students store their recent work and an assessment portfolio. Occasionally, a selection of work is transferred from the working portfolio to the assessment portfolio. Usually, the teacher provides some guidelines for what should be selected, allowing learners to choose within these guidelines.

Many teachers recommend that the number of entries in an assessment portfolio be limited. These entries provide a manageable but representative sample of work. New work can replace old, but some samples from throughout the year should remain.

Listed below are some ideas of representative work that might be included in such a portfolio:

- End-of-unit assessments
- Key assignments
- Student's solutions to challenging problems
- Written accounts of student's feelings about mathematics
- Drawings, sketches, and representations of mathematical ideas and situations
- Photographs of students engaging in mathematics
- Videotapes of students communicating mathematically

For more guidance on developing portfolio assessment, you may wish to consult one of several excellent sources listed on page 35. We especially recommend *Mathematics Assessment: Myths, Models, Good Questions, and Practical Suggestions,* edited by Jean Kerr Stenmark, available through the National Council of Teachers of Mathematics (NCTM). Portfolios, as well as other assessment issues, are also frequently addressed in the NCTM journal *Teaching Children Mathematics.* A video available from NCTM, *Mathematics Assessment: Alternative Approaches,* also discusses portfolios and may be helpful for teachers who are working together to develop a school-wide assessment policy.

◆ *Math Masters*, p. 474

# Ideas in the *Teacher's Lesson Guide*

***Portfolio Ideas*** Samples of students' work may be obtained from the following assignments:

## Unit 1
- Completing a Timed Inventory Test (**Lesson 1.5**)
- Identifying Properties of Kites and Rhombuses (**Lesson 1.5**)
- Designing a Compass (**Lesson 1.6**)
- Creating Circle Designs (**Lesson 1.6**)
- Creating Circle Designs (**Lesson 1.7**)
- Drawing Tangent Circles (**Lesson 1.7**)
- Inscribing an Equilateral Triangle in a Circle (**Lesson 1.8**)
- Construct a Kite (**Lesson 1.9**)
- Complete a Timed Inventory of Addition and Subtraction Facts (**Lesson 1.9**)

## Unit 2
- Completing Name-Collection Boxes (**Lesson 2.2**)
- Writing Addition Number Stories (**Lesson 2.7**)
- Writing Subtraction Number Stories (**Lesson 2.9**)
- Describe an Addition Strategy (**Lesson 2.10**)
- Describe a Subtraction Strategy (**Lesson 2.10**)
- Play *Name That Number* (**Lesson 2.10**)

## Unit 3
- Writing and Solving Number Stories about Air Distances (**Lesson 3.6**)
- Solving and Writing Number Stories (**Lesson 3.7**)
- Writing Open Sentences (**Lesson 3.10**)
- Creating Logic Puzzles (**Lesson 3.11**)
- Take a 50-Facts Test (**Lesson 3.12**)
- Write and Solve Number Stories (**Lesson 3.12**)

## Unit 4
- Writing Decimal Riddles (**Lesson 4.2**)
- Writing Number Stories (**Lesson 4.4**)
- Searching for Superlatives for Metric Units of Length (**Lesson 4.7**)
- Designing a Measurement Scavenger Hunt (**Lesson 4.8**)
- Writing and Solving Place-Value Puzzles (**Lesson 4.10**)
- Write and Solve Number Stories (**Lesson 4.11**)
- Describe a Problem-Solving Strategy (**Lesson 4.11**)

**Name** _____ **Date** _____

**Number-Story Math Log**

1. Write an easy number story that uses mathematical ideas that you have studied recently. Solve the problem.

   Number Story _____

   Solution _____

2. Write a difficult number story that uses mathematical ideas that you have studied recently. If you can, solve the number story. If you are not able to solve it, explain what you need to know to solve it.

   Number Story _____

   Solution _____

472                                    Use as needed.

© 2002 Everyday Learning Corporation

**ASSESSMENT MASTER**

✦ *Math Masters, p. 472*

## Unit 5

- Writing and Solving Multiplication Number Stories with Multiples of 10 **(Lesson 5.1)**
- Solving a Traveling Salesperson Problem **(Lesson 5.3)**
- Writing and Solving Multiplication Number Stories **(Lesson 5.5)**
- Judging a *Multiplication Wrestling* Competition **(Lesson 5.6)**
- Estimating the Number of Dots and the Weight of Paper Needed to Fill the Classroom **(Lesson 5.8)**
- Comparing Marathon Data **(Lesson 5.10)**
- Describe a Multiplication Strategy **(Lesson 5.12)**
- Solve Estimation Problems **(Lesson 5.12)**

## Unit 6

- Taking the Calculator Challenge **(Lesson 6.3)**
- Write and Solve Multiplication and Division Number Stories **(Lesson 6.11)**
- Describe a Division Strategy **(Lesson 6.11)**
- Measure Angles with a Circular and Half-Circle Protractor **(Lesson 6.11)**

## Unit 7

- Constructing an Equilateral Triangle **(Lesson 7.1)**
- Writing and Solving "Fraction-of" Number Stories **(Lesson 7.2)**
- Drawing and Comparing Line Segments **(Lesson 7.4)**
- Naming Fractional Parts of a Region **(Lesson 7.10)**
- Comparing Actual and Expected Results of 1,000 Cube Drops **(Lesson 7.12)**
- Describe a Fraction Addition or Subtraction Strategy **(Lesson 7.13)**

## Unit 8

- Making a Scale Drawing of Your Bedroom **(Lesson 8.2)**
- Constructing Figures with a Compass and Straightedge **(Lesson 8.6)**
- Comparing Areas **(Lesson 8.7)**
- Using Division to Compare Numbers of Mammal Species **(Lesson 8.8)**
- Find the Area and Perimeter of an Irregular Figure **(Lesson 8.9)**
- Make Enlargements **(Lesson 8.9)**
- Solve Perimeter and Area Problems **(Lesson 8.9)**

## Unit 9

- Making a Percent Booklet **(Lesson 9.1)**
- Writing and Solving "Percent-of" Number Stories **(Lesson 9.2)**
- Solving Challenging Discount Number Stories **(Lesson 9.4)**
- Graphing Survey Results **(Lesson 9.6)**
- Ranking Countries and Coloring a Map to Show Literacy Data **(Lesson 9.7)**
- Writing and Solving Division Number Stories with Decimals **(Lesson 9.9)**
- Find the "Fraction-of" and "Percent-of" a Design **(Lesson 9.10)**
- Describe a Decimal Division Strategy **(Lesson 9.10)**
- Describe a Decimal Multiplication Strategy **(Lesson 9.10)**

## Unit 10

- Creating a Paint Reflection **(Lesson 10.2)**
- Displaying Pictures of Symmetric Objects **(Lesson 10.4)**
- Exploring Turn Symmetry **(Lesson 10.4)**
- Creating Frieze Patterns **(Lesson 10.5)**
- Interpret a Cartoon **(Lesson 10.7)**

## Unit 11

- Comparing Mammals' Weights **(Lesson 11.1)**
- Writing and Solving "What Am I?" Riddles **(Lesson 11.3)**
- Exploring Volume by Building Prisms **(Lesson 11.5)**
- Estimating the Volume of a Sheet of Paper **(Lesson 11.5)**
- Modeling the Capacity of Annual Rice Consumption **(Lesson 11.7)**
- Solving a Record Rainfall Problem **(Lesson 11.8)**

## Unit 12

- Collecting Follow-Up Data on Eye-Blinking Rates **(Lesson 12.1)**
- Solving More Rate Problems **(Lesson 12.2)**
- Solving Mammal Speeds Problems **(Lesson 12.2)**
- Solving Mammal Heart Rates Problems **(Lesson 12.3)**
- Analyzing Data **(Lesson 12.3)**
- Calculating Unit Prices **(Lesson 12.5)**
- Comparing Prices **(Lesson 12.5)**
- Solve Multi-Step Problems Involving Rates **(Lesson 12.7)**

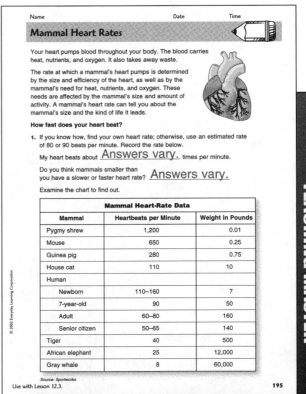

Name                    Date                    Time

**Mammal Heart Rates**

Your heart pumps blood throughout your body. The blood carries heat, nutrients, and oxygen. It also takes away waste.

The rate at which a mammal's heart pumps is determined by the size and efficiency of the heart, as well as by the mammal's need for heat, nutrients, and oxygen. These needs are affected by the mammal's size and amount of activity. A mammal's heart rate can tell you about the mammal's size and the kind of life it leads.

**How fast does your heart beat?**

1. If you know how, find your own heart rate; otherwise, use an estimated rate of 80 or 90 beats per minute. Record the rate below.

   My heart beats about  Answers vary.  times per minute.

   Do you think mammals smaller than you have a slower or faster heart rate?  Answers vary.

   Examine the chart to find out.

| Mammal Heart-Rate Data | | |
|---|---|---|
| **Mammal** | **Heartbeats per Minute** | **Weight in Pounds** |
| Pygmy shrew | 1,200 | 0.01 |
| Mouse | 650 | 0.25 |
| Guinea pig | 280 | 0.75 |
| House cat | 110 | 10 |
| Human | | |
| Newborn | 110–160 | 7 |
| 7-year-old | 90 | 50 |
| Adult | 60–80 | 160 |
| Senior citizen | 50–65 | 140 |
| Tiger | 40 | 500 |
| African elephant | 25 | 12,000 |
| Gray whale | 8 | 60,000 |

Source: Sportworks

Use with Lesson 12.3.                    195

© 2002 Everyday Learning Corporation

**TEACHING MASTER**

◆ *Math Masters,* p. 195

**Your Assessment Ideas**

_____

_____

_____

_____

_____

_____

_____

_____

_____

_____

_____

_____

_____

_____

_____

_____

_____

_____

_____

_____

_____

_____

_____

_____

_____

**Your Assessment Ideas**

# Rubrics

As most teachers know, learning and understanding are ongoing processes. One good way to keep track of each student's progress is to use a rubric. A rubric is a framework that helps you categorize progress on various aspects of a student's learning. A simple but effective rubric that many teachers use is the classification of students as Beginning, Developing, or Secure with respect to a particular skill or concept. The following rubrics are provided as an introduction to this topic. The most effective rubrics will be those that you and your fellow grade-level teachers tailor to the needs of your students and to the content you are covering.

---

### Sample Rubric

**Beginning (B)**
Students' responses have fragments of appropriate material and show effort to accomplish the task. Students do not explain either the concepts or procedures involved.

**Developing (D)**
Students accomplish part of the task independently. Students can partially explain the process but may need prompting to complete it.

**Secure (S)**
Students' strategies and executions meet the demands of the task and demonstrate a firm grasp of the concepts and procedures involved. Their responses also demonstrate a broad range of understanding, and students apply their understanding in different contexts.

---

Your own rubric can be modeled after the sample but tailored to meet individual tasks. The sample rubric above can be easily used with any of the sample assessment tools to keep track of the progress of individual students as well as the whole class. You may wish to use the symbols B, D, and S or another set of symbols, such as −, ✓, and +, to chart progress. One teacher suggests using red, yellow, and green color symbols. No matter which rubric symbols you use, a quick look at a completed Class Checklist or a Class Progress Indicator can tell you which areas need further review or which students will benefit from additional help or challenges.

Because some students fall between Developing and Secure or may show exemplary understanding, a 3-point rubric may seem insufficient for some areas you wish to assess. This may be especially true when you are examining performance on a Project or other larger activity. A general five-level rubric follows:

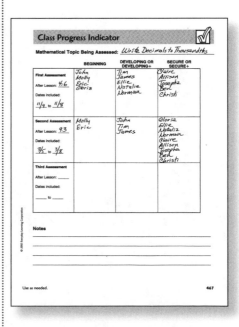

## Sample Rubric

**Beginning (B)**
Students' responses have fragments of appropriate material and show effort to accomplish the task. Students do not explain either the concepts or procedures involved.

**Developing (D)**
Students accomplish part of the task independently. Students can partially explain the process but may need prompting to complete it.

**Developing+ (D+)**
Responses convince you that students can revise the work to a Secure performance with the help of feedback (i.e., teacher prompts). While there is a basic understanding, it is not quite Secure or completely independent.

**Secure (S)**
Students' strategies and executions meet the demands of the task and demonstrate a firm grasp of the concepts and procedures involved. Their responses also demonstrate a broad range of understanding, and students apply their understanding in different contexts.

**Secure+ (S+)**
A Secure+ performance is exciting. In addition to meeting the qualifications for Secure, a student also merits distinction for special insights, good communication and reasoning, or other exceptional qualities.

Remember, the rubrics are only a framework. When you wish to use a rubric, the general indicators should be made more specific to fit the task, the time of the year, and the grade level at which the rubric is being used. An example of a rubric applied to a specific task is illustrated in this book in the section on Class Progress Indicators beginning on page 24.

Finally, another example of a general rubric follows. This rubric might be applied to a problem in which students are asked both to find an answer and to explain (or illustrate) their reasoning.

Rubrics such as these can be used to assess not only individual performance but also group processes for problem-solving tasks.

## Sample Rubric

**Level 0**
No attempts are made to solve the problem.

**Level 1**
Partial attempts are made. Reasoning is not explained. Problems are misunderstood or little progress is made.

**Level 2**
Students arrive at solutions, but solutions are incorrect. However, students clearly show reasoning and correct processes.
*or:*
Solutions are correct with little or no explanation given.

**Level 3**
Solutions are correct. Explanations are attempted but are incomplete.

**Level 4**
Solutions are correct. Explanations are clear and complete.

**Level 5**
Students give exemplary solutions.

# Ongoing Assessment

## Observing Students

Observing students during regular classroom interactions, as they work alone and in groups, is an important assessment technique in *Everyday Mathematics*. The methods described can help you manage ongoing observations. A discussion of record-keeping follows.

### Teacher-Guided Instruction

During the lesson, circulate around the room, interacting with the students and observing the mathematical behavior that is taking place. Identify those students who are having difficulty or showing progress. Be alert to significant comments and interactions. These quick observations often tell a great deal about a student's mathematical thinking. Practice making mental notes on the spot, and follow them up with brief written notes when possible. The important thing is to find an efficient way to keep track of students' progress without getting overwhelmed with papers, lists, and notes.

### Mathematical Mini-Interviews

Observing and listening to students as they work will enable you to note progress. However, there are times when brief verbal interactions with probing questions clarify and enhance observations. These brief, nonthreatening, one-on-one interactions, overheard by the rest of the class or conducted in private, encourage mathematical communication skills. They should apply to the content at hand during any instructional interaction.

### Games

At the beginning of the year, when children are first becoming comfortable with *Everyday Mathematics* games, and while they are working in small groups, circulate around the classroom observing the strategies that students are employing. Once students are playing the games independently, use the time to work with a small group having difficulty. Use recording tools to note any valuable information regarding individual mathematical development. You can also use this time to conduct mathematical mini-interviews.

### Mental Math and Reflexes

As you present the class with Mental Math and Reflexes situations, focus on a small group of students, perhaps five at a time. You should never feel that all students need to be observed every day.

### Strategy Sharing

Over time, encourage each student to share his or her strategies while working at the board or overhead projector. It is during this time that you should assume the role of "guide on the side" rather than "sage on the stage." In the *Everyday Mathematics* classroom, many strategies are used; recording students' strategies will help you know how to address individual strengths and needs.

### Slates

Periodically, record students' responses from their slate reviews. The *Teacher's Lesson Guide* offers suggested problems. You may begin with these problems or make up your own. Slate assessment offers both review and a quick assessment of students' progress toward computation mastery. You might focus on one group at a time and indicate only those students with Beginning understanding. Provide follow-up instruction for them based on your records.

## Recording Observations

When observing students, you may use a number of recording tools to organize your observations. The following suggestions may be helpful to you. Choose one that appeals to you most and try it. If necessary, adapt it to make it more useful or try another tool.

### Computer Labels

Print out students' names on sheets of large computer address labels. Write observations on the appropriate labels. As labels become filled, place them on numbered file cards and file them sequentially throughout the year.

### Seating Charts or Calendar Grids

Place each student's name in a grid cell and write observations in the cells as you circulate throughout the classroom. After reflecting on whole-class needs, cut apart the cells, date them, and file them for each student. Or use self-stick notes in the cells. Replace full notes with new ones to avoid having to cut out cells. Use the notes to analyze individual strengths and needs and to prepare for parent conferences.

### Class Checklists

A blank Class Checklist is provided in *Math Masters,* page 466. A mini version is shown on page 4 of this book. You may want to use it for recording ongoing observations and interactions by identifying a particular learning goal and using a rubric symbol to indicate students' progress on the checklist.

# Product Assessment

## Products from *Everyday Mathematics*

Samples of students' mathematical writings, drawings, and creations add balance to the assessment process. This section offers a review of some of the products that are part of *Everyday Mathematics,* as well as suggestions for outside sources for product assessment. Some of these items can be selected and stored in a portfolio or work folder along with other assessments.

### Math Journals

*Math Journals* can be considered working portfolios. Students should keep the journals intact so that they can revisit, review, correct, and improve their responses at a later time. You and students might select journal pages focusing on topics of concern or story problems or those featuring open-ended tasks to photocopy and include in portfolios. Some journal pages can be used to record information about long-term projects and reports on World Tour activities. You may access these pages to document students' progress on number collections, equivalent names for fractions, and scores on 50-facts tests. Two other types of journal pages that can be used as assessment are Math Boxes and Time to Reflect.

### Math Boxes

Math Boxes are an important routine for reviewing and maintaining skills. They also offer an excellent opportunity for ongoing assessment, providing glimpses into how a student performs in several areas. References in the *Teacher's Lesson Guide* identify paired Math Boxes pages and tell which problems cover prerequisites for the next unit.

One method for record keeping when assessing work with Math Boxes is to circulate and make informal observations on a copy of the Math Boxes page. Record names and comments about individuals who are having difficulties on self-stick notes placed over individual Math Boxes.

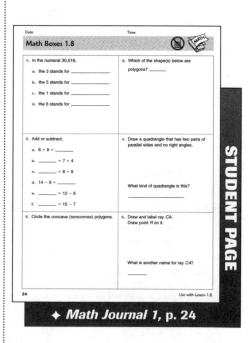

◆ *Math Journal 1, p. 24*

STUDENT PAGE

### Time to Reflect

These self-assessment journal pages offer students an opportunity to reflect on their progress. These single-page activities include two or three open-ended questions that lead students to decide which concepts they are finding easy, difficult, or surprising. Students might be asked how they would teach a concept or skill. Some questions simply ask students to critique their own performance. Student responses on these pages can provide a useful insight into students' mathematical reasoning skills.

## Additional Assessment Products

Many teachers are interested in gathering examples of students' writing and thinking in addition to those provided by *Everyday Mathematics* materials. This type of writing is usually more open-ended and allows teachers more flexibility in topics while they provide students with opportunities to reflect on, assess their understanding, and enhance their communication skills. This section provides examples of products you may wish to include in your assessment plan.

### Math Logs

Some teachers find it beneficial for students to write about mathematics regularly. A spiral notebook or a set of log sheets can be used as a math log. (See sample masters in *Math Masters*, pages 470–472.) Not only can these written reflections serve as a powerful means of checking students' understanding, but they are also a means of assessing curiosity, persistence, risk taking, and self-confidence.

Remember that math logs are not "end products" but, instead, are an important part of the ongoing assessment process referred to in the introduction. They are helpful to both you and students only if they reveal useful feedback and encourage the development of mathematical thinking, understanding, and written communication.

---

Name _____  Date _____

**Weekly Math Log** ✓

1. What did you study in math this week?

   *We worked on multiplication problems. I liked them.*

2. Many ideas in math are related to other ideas within math. Think about how the topic(s) you studied in class this week relate to other topics you learned before.

   Your reflection can include what you learned in previous years.

   *multiplication is related to division because it is the opposite.*

470                                            Use as needed.

Here are some suggestions on how to encourage students to write:

**Open-Ended Questions** Use open-ended questions to start students writing. Some prompts that you can use are

• *What does the term (range, landmark, square root) mean?*

• *What is (division, π)? Give an example of when you use it.*

• *Why is this answer right (wrong)? Explain.*

• *How do you know your answer is correct?*

• *What was your strategy for finding the solution?*

• *How many ways can you find a solution for this problem?*

• *Find the error in the following problem. Why is it an error?*

• *How is this like something you have learned before?*

Students may use Exit Slip sheets to record responses to open-ended questions at the close of a lesson or unit. (See *Math Masters*, page 475.)

**Number Stories** Occasionally ask students to write a number story. Sometimes you may wish to supply the numbers. For example:

• *Write a number story that uses the numbers $\frac{2}{3}$ and 0.5.*

• *Write a number story that uses all square numbers less than 10.*

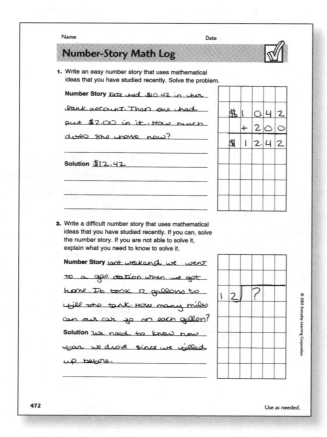

At other times, you may leave the instructions more open-ended:

• *Make up a number story using square units.*

• *Write a number story that uses a variable.*

Written number stories provide concrete assessment of students' understanding of operations, relationships, and numbers. For example, students might choose the incorrect operation to find an answer. Number stories often point out misconceptions.

**Portfolio Writing** If you are using portfolios, students can write entries for their portfolios. To help focus the writing, you might suggest that they write about one of the following topics:

• *What I Hope to Learn about Mathematics This Year*

• *Why Mathematics Is Important*

• *My Plan for Learning Mathematics*

As the year continues and entries change, ask students to update their introductions and tell why they have chosen the different pieces. At the end of the year, students could re-evaluate their portfolios and make a list of important concepts that they have learned.

**Concept and Strategy Writing** Prior to the teaching of a unit, invite students to share what they already know about the concepts being presented. For example, before you teach a unit on division, students could reflect in response to these questions or topics:

• *What is division?*

• *When do you use division?*

• *Write an example of the toughest kind of division problem you can solve. Then solve the problem.*

• *Write an example of a division number story.*

The answers to these questions/statements may help you plan your instruction. At the close of each unit, ask students to respond to the same statements or questions. This technique allows students and you to compare growth in understanding of the concepts. You may even discover a need to clear up some students' misconceptions.

Students can use words, representations, or both to explain their thinking. Communicating about mathematics encourages students to reflect upon their thinking and provides you with another window into their thought processes. Model this kind of writing on the overhead to show students how to use this format.

## Alternatives to Math Logs

Even if you do not want to have students keep regular math logs, have them occasionally write about mathematics so they can develop their writing skills. During each unit, give students short writing assignments. Writing topics can be based on any of the math log suggestions given, or they can be short reflections written just before the end-of-unit assessment. For example:

• *The math I know best/least in this unit is* _____.

• *Uses for the mathematics I learned in this unit are* _____.

These assignments could also be more content-oriented. For example:

• *Choose one of the geometric solids provided and describe its properties.*

• *Explain how to use the scale of a map.*

• *Describe the significance of the landmarks of a set of data.*

Try to include students in the assessment process. The products listed below will encourage students to develop their ability to think reflectively. These products can be used as Math Messages or Math Boxes within the program or in math logs or alternatives to math logs.

## Reflective Writing and Self-Assessment

Open-ended statements and questions, such as those suggested here, provide students with opportunities to reflect on what they know and what they do not know. Invite students to reflect before, during, and/or after a lesson. Here are some prompts you can use:

• *My goal for tomorrow is ...*

• *I learned that ...*

• *I was surprised that I ...*

• *I was pleased that I ...*

• *I still don't understand ...*

• *Because of the mathematics lesson today, I feel more confident about ...*

• *The most important thing I learned in* Everyday Mathematics *today (this week) is ...*

• *I think (percents, calculators) are ...*

• *(Multiplication) is easy if ...*

• *The trouble with mathematics is ...*

• *What I like most (or least) about Lesson X is ...*

• *How would you explain to an absent student what we did today?*

• *What was the most difficult (easiest) part of today's lesson?*

• *Write a test problem that I might give to see if you understand today's lesson.*

• *What did you learn today that you did not know before?*

• *What did you like or dislike about today's lesson? Why?*

NOTE: Do not feel discouraged if students have difficulty communicating mathematically. This is a skill that takes time to develop.

Students who begin the year having nothing to say or who answer in short, incomplete sentences become much more fluent as the year progresses.

How often should you use a math log or other writing in your math program? This depends on you and your students. While some teachers use logs a few times per week, you may find that once a week (perhaps on Friday, reflecting on what students did that week) or at the end of the unit is sufficient.

Choose the amount of additional writing with which you and your students feel comfortable.

Sometimes you may want students to focus on how they worked in a small group:

- *What worked well in your group today?*
- *Describe what your job was in your group today.*
- *What could you have done to help your group work better?*
- *What do you like or dislike about working in a group?*

**End-of-Year Reflection** This kind of writing may give teachers some ideas about students' attitudes toward mathematics and about which experiences have been the most beneficial. Responses will vary, depending on the writing ability and reflective experiences of the students.

I have learned a lot in math class this year. Now I can see why we had to learn addition and subtraction facts in 3rd grade. The facts are so easy to me now when I need to use them. I can do my problems faster.

One of my favorite things is geometry. There are so many things I see everyday that remind me of geometry. I see road signs, balls, kites, baseball diamonds and even buildings that remind me of geometry. Math is more than just numbers.

I learn a lot in math class when we play games. Name that Number is fun. And I like the riddles. My friends like to read them.

Many things help me learn math, but I think our journals are good because I can see all my work. The math boxes help me practice and review what I learn. And I like to bring study links home to show my family what I learn in class.

# Periodic Assessment

Periodic assessment activities are those that are done at fairly consistent times or intervals over the school year. We will briefly review periodic assessment sources that are currently part of *Everyday Mathematics* and then discuss additional sources that experienced teachers use.

## Sources from *Everyday Mathematics*

### Unit Reviews and Assessments

Each unit of your *Teacher's Lesson Guide* ends with a review and assessment lesson that lists the learning goals for that unit. The goals list is followed by a cumulative review that includes suggestions for oral and slate assessments as well as group or independent written assessment ideas and performance assessment activities. Assessment lessons also include a self-assessment page called "Time to Reflect" in students' journals.

This cumulative oral, slate, and written review provides an opportunity for you to check students' progress on concepts and skills that were introduced or further developed in the unit. In addition to these resources, other suggestions include

- Use rubrics to record progress toward each learning goal you assess. Rubrics are introduced on pages 13 and 14 of this book, and examples of how to use them are provided on pages 24–26 and in the unit Assessment Overviews section beginning on page 37.

- Only a few of the concepts and skills from any unit are suggested for assessment at the end of each unit. You should feel free to add items that you believe need assessing. You may also wish to delete items with which students are Secure.

- Since many of the end-of-unit reviews and assessments tend to focus on skills, you may want to add more concept-oriented and open-ended questions as suggested in the Product Assessment section of this book, beginning on page 17.

- You could accumulate information from the skills lists (in the review and assessment lessons) and then add them to the Quarterly Class Checklists and Individual Profiles of Progress.

### Assessing Students' Journal Work

You might use rubrics to periodically assess pages within journals as independent reviews. Also, several activities throughout the journals have students glue their best work onto the page. You might develop a rubric to assess these activities as well.

By recording your individual objectives on a Class Progress Indicator or a Class Checklist, you can ascertain which students may need additional experience. These students can then be paired with students who are proficient in that particular skill or activity.

### Midyear and End-of-Year Assessments

The Midyear and End-of-Year Assessment Masters (*Math Masters,* pages 415–425) provide additional assessment opportunities that you may wish to use as part of your balanced assessment plan. Minis of these masters, with answers, are shown on pages 91–96 of this book. These tests cover important concepts and skills presented in Fourth Grade *Everyday Mathematics,* but they are not designed to be used as "pretests," and they should not be your primary assessment tools. Use them along with the ongoing, product, and periodic assessments that are found within the lessons and at the end of each unit.

## Additional Sources for Periodic Assessment

### Class Progress Indicators

Class Progress Indicators, also known as Performance Charts, are another assessment tool that some teachers have found useful in assessing and tracking students' progress on selected mathematical topics.

A Class Progress Indicator form provides space to record students' performance on any mathematical topic you choose to assess two or three times during the year.

The first assessment opportunity, which usually occurs after students have some exposure to and experience with a topic, provides a baseline for your students' performance early in the year. By recording the second and third assessments on the same form, you can track the progress of each student as well as the whole class throughout the school year. A fourth grade teacher's sample Class Progress Indicator is shown on page 25. A blank form of this master is provided in *Math Masters,* page 467.

## Class Progress Indicator

**Mathematical Topic Being Assessed:** _Write Decimals to Thousandths_

| | BEGINNING | DEVELOPING OR DEVELOPING+ | SECURE OR SECURE+ |
|---|---|---|---|
| **First Assessment**<br><br>After Lesson: _4.6_<br><br>Dates included:<br><br>_11/4_ to _11/8_ | John<br>Molly<br>Eric<br>Gloria | Tim<br>James<br>Ellie<br>Natalia<br>Norman | Claire<br>Allison<br>Josepha<br>Ben<br>Christi |
| **Second Assessment**<br><br>After Lesson: _9.3_<br><br>Dates included:<br><br>_3/5_ to _3/8_ | Molly<br>Eric | John<br>Tim<br>James | Gloria<br>Ellie<br>Natalia<br>Norman<br>Claire<br>Allison<br>Josepha<br>Ben<br>Christi |
| **Third Assessment**<br><br>After Lesson: _____<br><br>Dates included:<br><br>_____ to _____ | | | |

**Notes**

_____

_____

_____

_____

Use as needed.                                                    467

Record the names of students under the columns that best indicate their ability levels: Beginning, Developing, or Secure, or whatever rubric symbols you like to use. If you wish, use (+) to indicate students who are between these levels. As you conduct your assessments, keep this question in mind: What do I need to do instructionally to promote progress? Space is provided at the bottom of the form for any notes you may wish to make.

Below is an example of a mathematical topic and an accompanying rubric.

Date                                    Time

### Modeling a Rectangular Prism

After you make a rectangular prism,
answer the questions below.

vertices

edges

faces

1. How many faces does your rectangular prism have? __6__ faces

2. How many of these faces are formed by rectangles? __6__ faces

3. How many of these faces are formed by squares? __0, or 2__ faces

4. Pick one of the faces. How many other faces are parallel to it? __1__ face(s)

5. How many edges does your rectangular prism have? __12__ edges

6. Pick an edge. How many other edges are parallel to it? __3__ edges

7. How many vertices does your rectangular prism have? __8__ vertices

8. Write T (true) or F (false) for each of the following statements
   about the rectangular prism you made.

   a. __T__ It has no curved surfaces.    b. __F__ It is a cylinder.

   c. __T__ All of the faces are polygons.    d. __F__ It has exactly four faces.

   e. __F__ All of the edges are parallel.    f. __T__ It has more vertices than faces.

**Challenge**

9. Draw a picture of your rectangular
   prism. You can show hidden edges
   with dashed lines (- - - - -).

310                                    Use with Lesson 11.2.

✦ *Math Journal 2*, p. 310

| Sample 3-Dimensional Geometry Rubric |
| --- |
| **Beginning (B)** |
| With the help of partners, students construct an appropriate prism and answer some questions correctly. Students do not freely use the terms *faces, edges, parallel,* or *vertices.* |
| **Developing (D)** |
| Students create a prism and answer most of the questions correctly on their own. Students use some of the lesson terms freely. Students may help each other answer some of the questions. |
| **Secure (S)** |
| Students can easily create a prism and answer the questions independently. Students use the lesson terms freely. Students may help others with the lesson. |

Remember, the more experience you have with the
range of students' responses, the easier it will be to determine or
assign rubrics.

## Class Checklists and Individual Profiles of Progress

To help you keep track of students' progress in areas that are important to your school and district, the authors of *Everyday Mathematics* have provided learning goals checklists for individuals and for the class. These Class Checklists and Individual Profiles of Progress are provided for each unit as well as for each quarter. They are found at the back of your *Math Masters* book on pages 426–463 and are reproduced in a reduced version in the Assessment Masters section of this book on pages 96–115.

The checklists identify learning outcomes for each unit of *Everyday Mathematics* and indicate the approximate level of proficiency expected: *Beginning, Developing,* or *Secure.* For many of the learning goals, the level is identified as "Developing" rather than "Secure." "Developing" topics have been included so that you can record student progress over time.

Many of these learning goals are assessed at the end of each unit; all of them are developed on journal pages. You may want to use the checklists to help you give priorities to lesson materials.

The checklists assume that students had *Everyday Mathematics* in Grades K–3. You may need to make adjustments for students who used other mathematics programs.

First, use the Class Checklists to gather and record information. Then, transfer selected information to the Individual Profiles of Progress sheet for each student's portfolio or for use during parent conferences.

The information recorded on the checklists can be obtained from end-of-unit oral and written assessments. In fact, you may want to bypass the Class Checklists and record this information from these assessments directly onto the Individual Profiles of Progress.

◆ **Math Masters, p. 446**

◆ **Math Masters, p. 447**

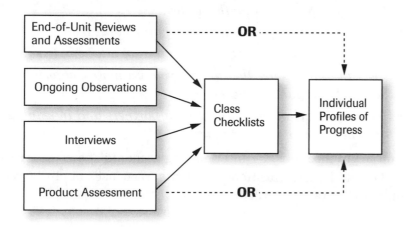

Blank profile and checklist masters can be found in *Math Masters,* pages 465 and 466. You may wish to record information from other sources, such as journal review pages, Math Boxes, Math Messages, and math logs.

Information obtained from teacher-directed instruction is also a good resource to be recorded on the Class Checklists or directly on Individual Profiles of Progress. As mentioned in the Ongoing Assessment section of this book, information can also be obtained from observations, questions, and other sources during regular instructional interactions.

## Individual Mathematical Interviews

Periodic interviews of ten to fifteen minutes with each student are a splendid idea and will prove valuable and revealing. They are, however, very difficult to carry out, given the full classroom schedule and the need to provide supervision for the rest of the class.

A compromise would be at least one goal-oriented, five-minute talk with each student during the year. At the start of the year, the interview might focus on the student's preparation for the content to come. At midyear, the interview might be concerned with how the work in mathematics has been going. Near the year's end, it might involve the student's preparation for next year.

The interview can be conducted while the rest of the class is playing mathematical games or working independently. Teachers have also suggested that, if it is feasible, you can make "appointments" to have lunch with students individually or with two or three students at a time. Other appointments might be arranged before class begins, during recess, or after school.

The following are suggested questions for a midyear interview:
- *How do you feel about mathematics?*
- *What have you enjoyed most about mathematics?*
- *What has been the easiest (hardest) part of mathematics for you?*
- *How can we work together to help you feel more comfortable with these difficult parts of mathematics?*
- *How do you feel about working with partners and in small groups for some mathematics activities?*

You might also consider interviewing students about their responses to Time to Reflect questions. Students' responses might be recorded on paper or tape-recorded.

## "My Math Class" Inventories

At the beginning of the year, you may want students to complete an inventory to assess their mathematical attitudes. This inventory might be repeated later in the year to see whether their attitudes have changed. Two samples (Evaluating My Math Class; My Math Class) are shown below. Blank masters of these inventories are found in *Math Masters,* pages 468 and 469. Inventories can be included in students' portfolios and discussed during individual interviews or parent conferences.

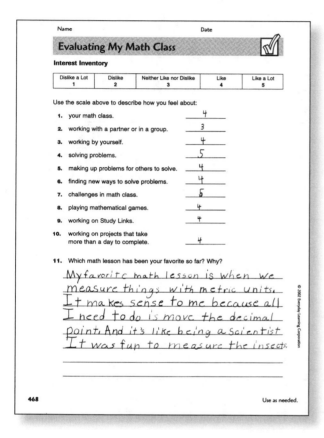

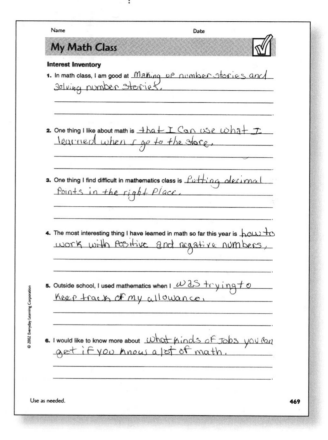

## Your Assessment Ideas

_____

_____

_____

_____

_____

_____

_____

_____

_____

_____

_____

_____

_____

_____

_____

_____

_____

_____

_____

_____

_____

_____

_____

_____

_____

_____

_____

_____

_____

_____

_____

_____

# Grading

Traditionally, the main purpose of end-of-unit assessments is to help the teacher monitor student progress and evaluate student achievement. In addition, end-of-unit assessments in *Everyday Mathematics* provide valuable information for planning future lessons.

The philosophy behind the end-of-unit assessments agrees with that expressed in the NCTM *Assessment Standards for School Mathematics* (1995). The diagram below, which is taken from that publication, illustrates how the four purposes of assessment translate into classroom practices:

**Four Purposes of Assessment and Their Results**

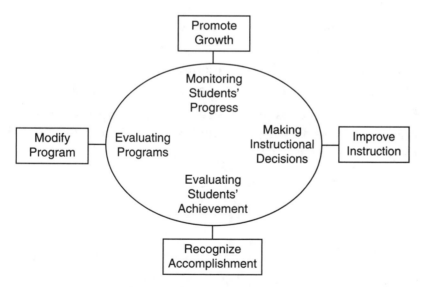

Because *Everyday Mathematics* presents concepts and skills repeatedly throughout the year, it is important to know how students are progressing individually on a concept or skill, as well as how much the class as a whole understands it. For that reason, the end-of-unit assessments in *Everyday Mathematics* include items at an exposure step of the spiral, in addition to items that assess mastery.

On the basis of students' performance on these assessment tools, teachers can make informed decisions about how to approach concepts and skills in future lessons. For example, several students may correctly answer a question on fraction addition, but the class as a whole is not Secure at it. The teacher knows that the next time the skill appears in the spiral, he or she can call on student leaders to help get the class started.

Since end-of-unit assessments have several purposes, they should not be the only source for grades. Following are some of the ways to accumulate scores for student grades:

- Create open-ended problems or use those that are in the journal. Grade the answers to these problems according to a rubric that assigns points to the different performance levels.
- Record scores on cumulative reviews.
- Record scores on review masters.
- Develop interim quizzes.
- Assign points for successful group problem solving.
- Weigh the value of questions on the end-of-unit assessments, checking progress according to your expectations for mastery.

This list is only a beginning. Assessment is as individual as are teaching styles. While developing your own assessment plan for *Everyday Mathematics,* consider the following guidelines:

- Start small.
- Define unit objectives to be assessed.
- Incorporate assessment into the class routine.
- Set up an easy and efficient record-keeping system.
- Personalize and adapt the plan as the year progresses.

*Everyday Mathematics* provides regular opportunities to assess student progress. Choose those that best match your teaching style and students' needs.

# Outside Tests

Outside tests are generally tests given at the school, district, or state level, or they are nationally standardized tests. Most teachers are familiar with the standardized tests that have multiple-choice responses. The frustrating aspect of this type of test is that it analyzes a narrow range of mathematical thinking and doesn't assess the depth and breadth of the mathematical knowledge that should be attained in a well-implemented *Everyday Mathematics* classroom.

There are ways to help your students function well in testing environments. Math Boxes, for example, can be tailored to help prepare students for the formats of an outside test. Even without such preparation, *Everyday Mathematics* students generally do about as well on the computation sections of standardized tests and much better on concepts and problem-solving sections, as students in traditional programs.

More recently, performance assessments or open-ended tests have been developed. These tests report results similar to those from traditional tests—class and individual norms (percentile rankings)—but they also attempt to test problem solving and communication skills on larger tasks. Some of these tests provide rubric scores along with normed data. Try to encourage the use of one of these newer performance-based tests at the district level rather than the traditional multiple-choice tests.

Performance-based assessments developed at the school or district level probably afford the best opportunity to reflect the instructional practices in local classrooms. Teams of teachers and administrators can develop assessments and rubrics that enhance the learning process rather than focus on narrow thinking used only in a small portion of mathematical activities. At some grade levels, these assessments can be used exclusively. When standardized testing is mandatory at a certain grade level, these assessments can give a better picture of the mathematical education occurring in the classroom.

## Your Assessment Ideas

_____

_____

_____

_____

_____

_____

_____

_____

_____

_____

_____

_____

_____

_____

_____

_____

_____

_____

_____

_____

_____

_____

_____

_____

_____

_____

_____

_____

_____

**Your Assessment Ideas**

# Recommended Reading

Black, Paul, and Dylan Wiliam. "Assessment and Classroom Learning." *Assessment in Education* (March, 1998): 7–74.

———. "Inside the Black Box: Raising Standards Through Classroom Assessment." *Phi Delta Kappan* 80, no. 2 (October, 1998): 139–149.

Bryant, Brian R., and Teddy Maddox. "Using Alternative Assessment Techniques to Plan and Evaluate Mathematics." *LD Forum* 21, no. 2 (winter, 1996): 24–33.

Eisner, Elliot W. "The Uses and Limits of Performance Assessment." *Phi Delta Kappan* 80, no. 9 (May, 1999): 658–661.

Kuhn, Gerald. *Mathematics Assessment: What Works in the Classroom*. San Francisco: Jossey-Bass Publishers, 1994.

National Council of Teachers of Mathematics (NCTM). *Curriculum and Evaluation Standards for School Mathematics*. Reston, Va.: NCTM, 1989.

———. *Assessment Standards for School Mathematics*. Reston, Va.: NCTM, 1995.

———. *Principles and Standards for School Mathematics*. Reston, Va.: NCTM, 2000.

National Research Council, Mathematical Sciences Education Board. *Measuring What Counts: A Conceptual Guide for Mathematics Assessment*. Washington, D.C.: National Academy Press, 1993.

Pearson, Bethyl, and Cathy Berghoff. "London Bridge Is Not Falling Down: It's Supporting Alternative Assessment." *TESOL Journal* 5, no. 4 (summer, 1996): 28–31.

Shepard, Lorrie A. "Using Assessment to Improve Learning." *Educational Leadership* 52, no. 5 (February, 1995): 38–43.

Stenmark, Jean Kerr, ed. *Mathematics Assessment: Myths, Models, Good Questions, and Practical Suggestions*. Reston, Va.: National Council of Teachers of Mathematics, 1991.

Stiggens, Richard J. *Student-Centered Classroom Assessment*. Englewood Cliffs, N.J.: Prentice-Hall, 1997.

Webb, N. L., and A. F. Coxford, eds. *Assessment in the Mathematics Classroom: 1993 Yearbook*. Reston, Va.: National Council of Teachers of Mathematics, 1993.

# Your Assessment Ideas

# Assessment Overviews

This section offers examples of how to use different types of assessments in specific lessons. For each unit, you will find examples of three major types of assessment opportunities: Ongoing Assessment, Product Assessment, and Periodic Assessment. Keep in mind, however, that these are not distinct categories; they frequently overlap. For example, some Periodic Assessments may also serve as Product Assessments that you or the student may choose to keep in the student's portfolio.

**Contents**      **Page**

# Unit 1
# Assessment Overview

There are many pathways to a balanced assessment plan. As you teach Unit 1, start to become familiar with some of the approaches to assessment. The next few pages provide examples of the three major types of assessment suggested in this program: Ongoing Assessment, Product Assessment, and Periodic Assessment. This assessment overview offers examples of ways to assess students on what they learn in Unit 1. Do not try to use all of the examples, but begin with a few that meet your needs.

## Ongoing Assessment Opportunities

Ongoing assessment provides opportunities to observe students during regular interactions as they work independently and in groups. You can conduct ongoing assessment during teacher-guided instruction, Math Boxes sessions, mathematical mini-interviews, games, Mental Math and Reflexes sessions, strategy sharing, and slate work. The chart below provides a summary of ongoing assessment opportunities in Unit 1 as they relate to specific Unit 1 learning goals.

| | |
|---|---|
| **1a** **Beginning Goal** Use a compass and straightedge to construct geometric figures. (Lessons 1.6 and 1.8) | Lesson 1.7, p. 49 |
| **1c** **Developing Goal** Classify quadrangles according to side and angle properties. (Lessons 1.3–1.5) | Lesson 1.3, p. 28 |
| **1g** **Secure Goal** Know addition and subtraction facts. (Lessons 1.1–1.5) | Lesson 1.5, p. 40 |

## Product Assessment Opportunities

*Math Journals,* Math Boxes, Activity Sheets, *Math Masters,* math logs, and the results of Projects all provide product assessment opportunities. On the next page is an example of how you might use a rubric to assess a student's ability to complete a timed inventory test.

**ALTERNATIVE ASSESSMENT** Completing a Timed Inventory
Test

Most of your students should have achieved mastery of
addition and subtraction facts in third grade. This test
will help you gauge mastery. Because they should know
the answers "by heart," students should not be given
enough time to *figure out* the answers. Compare students' results on
this test with results on the one provided at the end of this unit in
Lesson 1.9, page 61. Timed tests are just one means to assess
student fact automaticity. Keep in mind that some students may
know their facts "by heart" but are unable to complete the entire
page. The sample rubric below can help you evaluate students'
work.

| Sample Rubric |
| --- |
| **Beginning (B)**<br>The student has difficulty in answering "easy" and "more difficult" facts. He or she is still developing strategies or is using inefficient strategies to arrive at an answer. The student may know a few of the "easy" facts "by heart." |
| **Developing (D)**<br>The student knows most of the "easy" addition and subtraction facts "by heart" but still struggles with "more difficult" facts. He or she is still using strategies to arrive at an answer for those facts. |
| **Secure (S)**<br>The student knows "easy" and "more difficult" facts "by heart." The student completes most of the facts accurately in the allotted time. |

## Periodic Assessment Opportunities

Here is a summary of the periodic assessment opportunities that
are provided in Unit 1. Refer to Lesson 1.9 for details.

### *Oral and Slate Assessment*

In Lesson 1.9, you will find oral and slate assessment problems on
pages 58–60.

### *Written Assessment*

In Lesson 1.9, you will find written assessment problems on
page 60 (*Math Masters,* pp. 387–389).

See the following chart to find oral, slate, and written assessment
problems, as well as alternative assessment options that address
specific learning goals.

| | | |
|---|---|---|
| **1a** | **Beginning Goal** Use a compass and straightedge to construct geometric figures. (Lessons 1.6 and 1.8) | Alternative Assessment Option |
| **1b** | **Developing Goal** Identify properties of polygons. (Lessons 1.3–1.7) | Oral Assessment, Problem 1 Written Assessment, Problems 2, 7, and 8 |
| **1c** | **Developing Goal** Classify quadrangles according to side and angle properties. (Lessons 1.3–1.5) | Oral Assessment, Problem 1 Written Assessment, Problems 1, 3, 7, and 8 |
| **1d** | **Developing/Secure Goal** Name, draw, and label line segments, lines, and rays. (Lessons 1.2, 1.4, and 1.8) | Oral Assessment, Problem 2 Slate Assessment, Problems 2 and 3 Written Assessment, Problems 4–6 |
| **1e** | **Developing/Secure Goal** Name, draw, and label angles, triangles, and quadrangles. (Lessons 1.3–1.5 and 1.8) | Slate Assessment, Problem 4 Written Assessment, Problems 3 and 9 |
| **1f** | **Developing/Secure Goal** Identify and describe right angles, parallel lines, and line segments. (Lessons 1.2–1.4) | Oral Assessment, Problems 1 and 2 Slate Assessment, Problems 2–4 Written Assessment, Problems 3, 4, and 9 |
| **1g** | **Secure Goal** Know addition and subtraction facts. (Lessons 1.1–1.5) | Slate Assessment, Problem 1 Alternative Assessment Option |

## Alternative Assessment

In Lesson 1.9, you will find alternative assessment options on page 61.

### ✦ Construct a Kite

Assess a student's skill in using a compass and straightedge to construct a kite. Use Calendar Grids or a Class Checklist as you circulate. Consider the following questions:

• Has the student had sufficient practice using a compass? Some students require considerable practice to become proficient with a compass.

• Does the student keep the compass point anchored properly?

### ✦ Complete a Timed Inventory of Addition and Subtraction Facts

Use the same rubric for this test as you used for the one students completed in Lesson 1.5. Compare results for the two tests to gauge students' mastery of addition and subtraction facts.

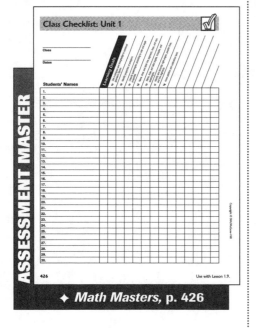

✦ *Math Masters, p. 426*

# Unit 2
# Assessment Overview

If you tried some of the assessment approaches that were suggested in the Unit 1 Assessment Overview, you are probably beginning to appreciate how the goal charts in this section can help you plan your assessment strategies. For example, at this point students are expected to be at a Secure level for giving equivalent names for numbers (see Goal 2g in the chart below). The chart alerts you to the fact that ongoing assessment opportunities related to that goal are provided in Lesson 2.2 on pages 84 and 85 of your *Teacher's Lesson Guide*. In similar fashion, you can use the chart on page 43 to find slate, written, and alternative assessment opportunities related to this same goal.

## Ongoing Assessment Opportunities

Ongoing assessment provides opportunities to observe students during regular interactions as they work independently and in groups. You can conduct ongoing assessment during teacher-guided instruction, Math Boxes sessions, mathematical mini-interviews, games, Mental Math and Reflexes sessions, strategy sharing, and slate work. The chart below provides a summary of ongoing assessment opportunities in Unit 2 as they relate to specific Unit 2 learning goals.

| | | |
|---|---|---|
| **2d** | **Secure Goal** Subtract multidigit numbers. (Lesson 2.9) | Lesson 2.9, p. 125 |
| **2e** | **Secure Goal** Add multidigit numbers. (Lessons 2.7 and 2.8) | Lesson 2.8, p. 118 |
| **2f** | **Developing/Secure Goal** Read and write numerals to hundred-millions; give the value of the digits in numerals to hundred-millions. (Lessons 2.3 and 2.4) | Lesson 2.4, p. 96 |
| **2g** | **Secure Goal** Find equivalent names for numbers. (Lessons 2.2 and 2.9) | Lesson 2.2, pp. 84 and 85 |

## Product Assessment Opportunities

*Math Journals,* Math Boxes, Activity Sheets, *Math Masters,* math logs, and the results of Projects all provide product assessment opportunities. Here is an example of how you might use a rubric to assess a student's ability to describe an addition strategy.

Lesson 2.10, p. 130

**ALTERNATIVE ASSESSMENT** **Describe an Addition Strategy**

Most of your students should be able to use several methods for addition, but ability levels will vary. Some students will prefer more traditional methods, whereas others will try the partial-sums method or the column-addition method introduced in Lesson 2.7. As you have students solve two addition problems independently, ask them to describe their solution strategies. Use your own rubric, or the sample rubric below, to evaluate students' work.

**Portfolio Ideas**

| Sample Rubric |
| --- |
| **Beginning (B)**<br>The student attempts to solve the addition problem with a response that displays fragments of appropriate procedures but shows effort toward a solution. It is evident that he or she is unsure of place-value concepts and has not developed a meaningful procedure. |
| **Developing (D)**<br>The student solves the addition problem correctly, but it is evident that he or she lacks complete understanding of place value or of the procedure used. As a result, the written solution strategy is unclear. |
| **Secure (S)**<br>The student solves the addition problem correctly, displaying clear place-value understanding, as well as how the selected procedure works. This is also evident in the solution strategy the student has written. |

## Periodic Assessment Opportunities

Here is a summary of the periodic assessment opportunities that are provided in Unit 2. Refer to Lesson 2.10 for details.

### *Oral and Slate Assessment*

In Lesson 2.10, you will find oral and slate assessment problems on pages 128 and 129.

### *Written Assessment*

In Lesson 2.10, you will find written assessment problems on pages 129 and 130 (*Math Masters,* pp. 390 and 391).

See the following chart to find oral, slate, and written assessment problems, as well as alternative assessment options that address specific learning goals.

| | | |
|---|---|---|
| **2a** | **Developing/Secure Goal** Display data with a line plot, bar graph, or tally chart. (Lessons 2.5, 2.6, and 2.8) | Written Assessment, Problem 14 |
| **2b** | **Developing Goal** Use the statistical landmarks median, mode, and range. (Lessons 2.5, 2.6, and 2.8) | Written Assessment, Problems 10–13 |
| **2c** | **Secure Goal** Use the statistical landmarks maximum and minimum. (Lessons 2.5, 2.6, and 2.8) | Written Assessment, Problems 8 and 9 |
| **2d** | **Secure Goal** Subtract multidigit numbers. (Lesson 2.9) | Slate Assessment, Problem 4 Written Assessment, Problems 5–7 Alternative Assessment Option |
| **2e** | **Secure Goal** Add multidigit numbers. (Lesson 2.7) | Written Assessment, Problems 2–4 Alternative Assessment Option |
| **2f** | **Developing/Secure Goal** Read and write numerals to hundred-millions; give the value of the digits in numerals to hundred-millions. (Lessons 2.3 and 2.4) | Oral Assessment, Problems 1 and 2 Slate Assessment, Problems 2 and 3 |
| **2g** | **Secure Goal** Find equivalent names for numbers. (Lesson 2.2) | Slate Assessment, Problem 1 Written Assessment, Problem 1 Alternative Assessment Option |

## Alternative Assessment

In Lesson 2.10, you will find alternative assessment options on pages 130 and 131.

### ✦ Describe an Addition Strategy

Use the suggestions on page 42 to assess a student's ability to describe an addition strategy.

### ✦ Describe a Subtraction Strategy

Develop a rubric similar to the sample rubric on page 42, but tailor it to focus on subtraction skills. Then, use your rubric to assess a student's ability to describe a subtraction strategy.

### ✦ Play *Name That Number*

As students work with partners to play the game, have them record the number models that they use. Use Calendar Grids or a Class Checklist as you circulate. Keep such questions as the following in mind:

- Does the student identify and use combinations of sums and differences that match a given number?
- Does the student identify and use combinations of products and quotients that match a given number?

**✦ Math Masters, p. 428**

# Unit 3
# Assessment Overview

The first four lessons of this unit provide students an opportunity to review and practice basic multiplication facts. At this stage in their learning, most of your fourth-grade students should be at a Secure level for solving basic multiplication facts (see Goal 3g in the chart below). In other words, they probably already know all of the multiplication facts, although they may have to take time to figure out some answers. The chart below indicates that three ongoing assessment opportunities related to this goal can be found in Lessons 3.1, 3.3, and 3.5 on pages 148, 159, and 170 of your *Teacher's Lesson Guide*. Similarly, the chart on page 46 indicates where you can find slate and written problems to assess students' progress toward this same goal.

## Ongoing Assessment Opportunities

Ongoing assessment provides opportunities to observe students during regular interactions as they work independently and in groups. You can conduct ongoing assessment during teacher-guided instruction, Math Boxes sessions, mathematical mini-interviews, games, Mental Math and Reflexes sessions, strategy sharing, and slate work. The chart below provides a summary of ongoing assessment opportunities in Unit 3 as they relate to specific Unit 3 learning goals.

| | |
|---|---|
| **3b** **Developing Goal** Understand the function and placement of parentheses in number sentences. (Lessons 3.9 and 3.10) | Lesson 3.9, p. 188 |
| **3c** **Developing Goal** Determine whether number sentences are true or false. (Lessons 3.8–3.10) | Lesson 3.8, p. 181 |
| **3f** **Developing Goal** Know division facts. (Lessons 3.4–3.6 and 3.9) | Lesson 3.5, p. 170 |
| **3g** **Developing/Secure Goal** Know multiplication facts. (Lessons 3.1–3.6 and 3.9) | Lesson 3.1, p. 148 <br> Lesson 3.3, p. 159 <br> Lesson 3.5, p. 170 |
| **3h** **Secure Goal** Understand the relationship between multiplication and division. (Lessons 3.4–3.6 and 3.9) | Lesson 3.4, p. 163 <br> Lesson 3.5, p. 170 |

# Product Assessment Opportunities

*Math Journals,* Math Boxes, Activity Sheets, *Math Masters,* math logs, and the results of Projects all provide product assessment opportunities. Here is an example of how you might use a rubric to assess a student's ability to write and solve number stories.

Lesson 3.12, p. 201

**ALTERNATIVE ASSESSMENT** Write and Solve Number Stories

A good way to assess students' abilities to apply their knowledge of addition, subtraction, multiplication, and division is to have them write number stories involving these operations and then solve them. *Math Masters,* page 48 (see mini in margin of this page), provides information from which students can create their number stories. Use your own rubric, or the sample rubric below, to evaluate students' work.

| Sample Rubric |
|---|
| **Beginning (B)** |
| The student writes a number story, but some assistance may be required. He or she may write a number story that is not connected to the data given or does not use the data appropriately. As a result, the number story does not make sense. The number model and answer are incorrect or not given. |
| **Developing (D)** |
| The student is able to write a single-step number story that is connected to the data given. The student may need assistance in solving the problem. A number model and correct answer are given. |
| **Secure (S)** |
| The student creates a number story using the data given. The number story may involve multisteps. A number model and correct answer are given. |

# Periodic Assessment Opportunities

Here is a summary of the periodic assessment opportunities that are provided in Unit 3. Refer to Lesson 3.12 for details.

## *Oral and Slate Assessment*

In Lesson 3.12, you will find oral and slate assessment problems on pages 199 and 200.

## *Written Assessment*

In Lesson 3.12, you will find written assessment problems on page 200 (*Math Masters,* pp. 392–394).

See the chart on the next page to find oral, slate, and written assessment problems that address specific learning goals.

✦ *Math Masters, p. 48*

| | | |
|---|---|---|
| **3a** **Developing Goal** Solve open sentences. (Lesson 3.10) | Written Assessment, Problems 18–23 |
| **3b** **Developing Goal** Understand the function and placement of parentheses in number sentences. (Lessons 3.9 and 3.10) | Written Assessment, Problems 8–17 |
| **3c** **Developing Goal** Determine whether number sentences are true or false. (Lessons 3.8–3.10) | Oral Assessment, Problem 1 Written Assessment, Problems 4–9 |
| **3d** **Developing/Secure Goal** Solve addition and subtraction number stories. (Lessons 3.7 and 3.11) | Written Assessment, Problems 24–27 |
| **3e** **Developing Goal** Use a map scale to estimate distances. (Lessons 3.6, 3.8, and 3.11) | Slate Assessment, Problem 2 Written Assessment, Problems 28 and 29 |
| **3f** **Developing Goal** Know division facts. (Lessons 3.4–3.6 and 3.9) | Slate Assessment, Problem 1 Written Assessment, Problems 2, 3, 6, 9, 12, 13, 15, 20, and 21 |
| **3g** **Developing/Secure Goal** Know multiplication facts. (Lessons 3.1–3.6 and 3.9) | Slate Assessment, Problem 1 Written Assessment, Problems 1, 4, 6–11, 13, 17, 19, and 23 |
| **3h** **Secure Goal** Understand the relationship between multiplication and division. (Lessons 3.4–3.6 and 3.9) | Slate Assessment, Problem 3 Written Assessment, Problems 1–3 |

## *Alternative Assessment*

In Lesson 3.12, you will find alternative assessment options on page 201.

### ✦ Take a 50-Facts Test

This test was introduced in Lesson 3.2 to help students develop speed and accuracy with basic multiplication facts. The test was to be administered about every three weeks, or more often if you wished. To assess their progress, have students graph their results from each of the tests.

### ✦ Write and Solve Number Stories

Use the suggestions and rubric on page 45 to assess a student's ability to write and solve multiplication number stories.

✦ *Math Masters, p. 430*

# Unit 4
# Assessment Overview

At this point in the *Everyday Mathematics* program, you may wish to consider whether you are beginning to establish a balance of Ongoing, Product, and Periodic Assessment strategies. Also, think about whether your strategies include both anecdotal records based on observations of students' progress and the use of written assessments.

## Ongoing Assessment Opportunities

Ongoing assessment provides opportunities to observe students during regular interactions as they work independently and in groups. You can conduct ongoing assessment during teacher-guided instruction, Math Boxes sessions, mathematical mini-interviews, games, Mental Math and Reflexes sessions, strategy sharing, and slate work. The chart below provides a summary of ongoing assessment opportunities in Unit 4 as they relate to specific Unit 4 learning goals.

| | | |
|---|---|---|
| **4c** | **Developing Goal** Read and write decimals to thousandths. (Lessons 4.1–4.6) | Lesson 4.1, p. 218<br>Lesson 4.6, p. 240 |
| **4f** | **Developing Goal** Use personal references to estimate lengths in metric units. (Lesson 4.8) | Lesson 4.8, p. 250 |
| **4g** | **Developing Goal** Solve 1- and 2-place decimal addition and subtraction problems and number stories. (Lessons 4.4 and 4.5) | Lesson 4.4, p. 229 |

## Product Assessment Opportunities

*Math Journals,* Math Boxes, Activity Sheets, *Math Masters,* math logs, and the results of Projects all provide produce assessment opportunities. On the next page is an example of how you might use a rubric to assess a student's ability to write and solve number stories.

Lesson 4.12, p. 264

**ALTERNATIVE ASSESSMENT** Write and Solve Number Stories

A good way to assess students' abilities to apply their knowledge of decimals is to have them write and solve number stories involving addition and subtraction of decimals. Use your own rubric, or the sample rubric below, to evaluate students' work.

| Sample Rubric |
|---|
| **Beginning (B)** |
| The student attempts to write a decimal number story, but some assistance may be required. The story is written, but it is not connected to decimals. |
| **Developing (D)** |
| The student writes a number story involving decimals with little or no assistance. The story includes a question and a unit such as money. The number model is written correctly, but the solution may be incorrect due to a lack of decimal place-value understanding. |
| **Secure (S)** |
| The student writes a number story that displays an understanding of decimals through the context of the story. The number model is written correctly and the solution is correct to reflect an understanding of decimal place value. |

## Periodic Assessment Opportunities

Here is a summary of the periodic assessment opportunities that are provided in Unit 4. Refer to Lesson 4.11 for details.

### Oral and Slate Assessment

In Lesson 4.11, you will find oral and slate assessment problems on pages 262 and 263.

### Written Assessment

In Lesson 4.11, you will find written assessment problems on pages 263 and 264 (*Math Masters,* pp. 395 and 396).

See the chart below to find oral, slate, and written assessment problems, as well as alternative assessment options that address specific learning goals.

| | | |
|---|---|---|
| **4a** | **Developing Goal** Express metric measures with decimals. (Lesson 4.9) | Slate Assessment, Problem 4<br>Written Assessment,<br>Problems 3, 4, 8, 9, 18, and 19 |
| **4b** | **Developing Goal** Convert between metric measures. (Lessons 4.7 and 4.9) | Slate Assessment, Problem 4<br>Written Assessment,<br>Problems 17–20 |
| **4c** | **Developing Goal** Read and write decimals to thousandths. (Lessons 4.1–4.6) | Oral Assessment, Problem 2<br>Slate Assessment,<br>Problems 1, 4, and 5<br>Written Assessment,<br>Problems 1 and 2 |
| **4d** | **Developing Goal** Compare and order decimals. (Lesson 4.2) | Written Assessment,<br>Problems 1, 6, and 12–16 |

| | | |
|---|---|---|
| **4e** **Developing Goal** Draw and measure line segments to the nearest millimeter. (Lesson 4.9) | Written Assessment, Problems 8–11 | |
| **4f** **Developing Goal** Use personal references to estimate lengths in metric units. (Lesson 4.8) | Written Assessment, Problems 3 and 4 Alternative Assessment Option | |
| **4g** **Developing Goal** Solve 1- and 2-place decimal addition and subtraction problems and number stories. (Lessons 4.4 and 4.5) | Oral Assessment, Problem 1 Slate Assessment, Problems 3 and 5 Written Assessment, Problems 14, 15, 21, and 22 Alternative Assessment Option | |
| **4h** **Secure Goal** Draw and measure line segments to the nearest centimeter. (Lesson 4.9) | Written Assessment, Problems 7 and 10 Alternative Assessment Option | |
| **4i** **Secure Goal** Use dollars-and-cents notation. (Lesson 4.5) | Slate Assessment, Problems 2 and 3 Written Assessment, Problems 5 and 22 Alternative Assessment Option | |

## Alternative Assessment

In Lesson 4.11, you will find alternative assessment options on pages 264 and 265.

### ✦ Estimate and Measure Lengths of Objects

Ask students to estimate the lengths, in metric units, of various objects that you put on display. They are to use their own personal references for common measure units. For example, a finger width may be about a centimeter. Once they have made an estimate, have them make actual measurements to the nearest centimeter. Use Calendar Grids or a Class Checklist as you circulate. Keep questions such as the following in mind:

• Does the student use appropriate references for metric units?

• Are the estimates reasonably accurate?

• Does the student use appropriate techniques to measure objects?

### ✦ Write and Solve Number Stories

Use the suggestions and rubric on page 48 to assess a student's ability to write and solve number stories involving addition and subtraction of decimals.

### ✦ Describe a Problem-Solving Strategy

Have students solve the decimal addition and subtraction problems that you made up in advance. Ask them to include descriptions of their solution strategies. Collect their work, and consider questions such as the following:

• Does the solution and strategy reflect understanding of addition or subtraction?

• Does the solution and strategy reflect a clear understanding of place-value concepts?

✦ *Math Masters*, p. 432

# Unit 5
# Assessment Overview

The focus of this unit is on multiplication computation and working with numbers to billions. The students should be developing several critical abilities related to multiplication and large numbers at this time (see Goals 5b–5f) and should be Secure in comparing large numbers (see Goal 5g). The goal chart below suggests ongoing assessment opportunities that you may wish to use. Slate, oral, and written assessments for these goals are suggested in the chart on pages 51 and 52. Further, keep in mind that games are used throughout *Everyday Mathematics* to reinforce students' memorization of basic multiplication facts.

## Ongoing Assessment Opportunities

Ongoing assessment provides opportunities to observe students during regular interactions as they work independently and in groups. You can conduct ongoing assessment during teacher-guided instruction, Math Boxes sessions, mathematical mini-interviews, games, Mental Math and Reflexes sessions, strategy sharing, and slate work. The chart below provides a summary of ongoing assessment opportunities in Unit 5 as they relate to specific Unit 5 learning goals.

| | | |
|---|---|---|
| **5b** | **Developing Goal** Know extended multiplication facts. (Lessons 5.1 and 5.2) | Lesson 5.1, p. 285<br>Lesson 5.4, p. 300 |
| **5c** | **Developing Goal** Make magnitude estimates for products of multidigit numbers. (Lesson 5.4) | Lesson 5.4, p. 300 |
| **5d** | **Developing Goal** Solve multidigit multiplication problems. (Lessons 5.2, and 5.5–5.7) | Lesson 5.2, p. 288<br>Lesson 5.4, p. 300<br>Lesson 5.6, p. 311 |
| **5e** | **Developing Goal** Round whole numbers to a given place. (Lessons 5.3, 5.4, and 5.10) | Lesson 5.10, p. 337 |
| **5f** | **Developing Goal** Read and write numbers to billions; name the values of digits in numerals to billions. (Lessons 5.8, 5.10, and 5.11) | Lesson 5.7, p. 320<br>Lesson 5.8, pp. 324<br>  and 325 |
| **5g** | **Secure Goal** Compare large numbers. (Lessons 5.8, 5.10, and 5.11) | Lesson 5.7, p. 320 |

# Product Assessment Opportunities

*Math Journals,* Math Boxes, Activity Sheets, *Math Masters,* math logs, and the results of Projects all provide product assessment opportunities. Below is an example of how you might use a rubric to assess a student's ability to describe a multiplication strategy.

Lesson 5.12, p. 348

**ALTERNATIVE ASSESSMENT** **Describe a Multiplication Strategy**

Most of your students should be able to use several methods for multiplying, but ability levels will vary. Some students will prefer finding partial products, whereas others will try the lattice method. Use your own rubric, or the sample rubric below, to evaluate students' work.

| Sample Rubric |
| --- |
| **Beginning (B)** |
| The student attempts to solve the multiplication problem with a response that displays only fragments of appropriate procedures but shows effort toward a solution. It is evident that he or she is unsure of place value concepts and has not developed a meaningful procedure. |
| **Developing (D)** |
| The student solves the multiplication problem correctly, but it is evident that he or she lacks understanding of place value or of the procedure used. The student is unable to articulate a clear understanding of the procedure used when writing about his or her solution strategy. |
| **Secure (S)** |
| The student solves the multiplication problem correctly and displays understanding of place value and how the selected procedure works. This is also evident in the solution strategy that the student writes. |

# Periodic Assessment Opportunities

Here is a summary of the periodic assessment opportunities that are provided in Unit 5. Refer to Lesson 5.12 for details.

## *Oral and Slate Assessment*

In Lesson 5.12, you will find oral and slate assessment problems on pages 346 and 347.

## *Written Assessment*

In Lesson 5.12, you will find written assessment problems on pages 347 and 348 (*Math Masters,* pp. 397 and 398).

See the chart below to find oral, slate, and written assessment problems, as well as alternative assessment options that address specific learning goals.

| | |
| --- | --- |
| **5a** **Beginning Goal** Use exponential notation to represent powers of 10. (Lesson 5.9) | Slate Assessment, Problem 5 Written Assessment, Problem 12 |
| **5b** **Developing Goal** Know extended multiplication facts. (Lessons 5.1 and 5.2) | Written Assessment, Problems 3, 4, 13, and 14 Alternative Assessment Option |

| | |
|---|---|
| **5c** **Developing Goal** Make magnitude estimates for products of multidigit numbers. (Lesson 5.4) | Oral Assessment, Problem 2<br>Written Assessment,<br>  Problems 2 and 19<br>Alternative Assessment Option |
| **5d** **Developing Goal** Solve multidigit multiplication problems. (Lessons 5.2 and 5.5–5.7) | Slate Assessment, Problem 3<br>Written Assessment,<br>  Problems 15–19<br>Alternative Assessment Option |
| **5e** **Developing Goal** Round whole numbers to a given place. (Lessons 5.3, 5.4, and 5.10) | Slate Assessment, Problem 4<br>Written Assessment,<br>  Problems 6–8 |
| **5f** **Developing Goal** Read and write numbers to billions; name the values of digits in numerals to billions. (Lessons 5.8, 5.10, and 5.11) | Oral Assessment, Problem 1<br>Slate Assessment,<br>  Problems 1 and 2 |
| **5g** **Secure Goal** Compare large numbers. (Lessons 5.8, 5.10, and 5.11) | Written Assessment,<br>  Problems 5 and 9–12 |
| **5h** **Secure Goal** Estimate sums. (Lesson 5.3) | Oral Assessment, Problem 2<br>Written Assessment, Problem 1 |

## Alternative Assessment

In Lesson 5.12, you will find alternative assessment options on page 348.

### ✦ Solve Computation Tile Problems

Use *Math Masters*, p. 89, to assess students' number sense, understanding of place value, and addition and subtraction computation. As students work independently to solve the problems, keep the following questions in mind:

• Can the student distinguish between odd and even numbers?

• Does the student understand *largest possible sum, smallest possible sum,* and so on.

• Is the student able to decide what to do to solve the problems with little or no direction?

### ✦ Describe a Multiplication Strategy

Use the multiplication rubric on p. 51 to assess how well students can multiply multidigit numbers.

### ✦ Solve Bank Robber Problems

As students work in pairs to solve these problems, circulate and observe. Assess their problem-solving skills as well as their abilities to estimate and work with large numbers.

• Are the partners able to come up with reasonable solutions that they can support?

• Could the partners estimate with fractions?

• Did the partners know how to compare 1 million minutes and 1 thousand weeks?

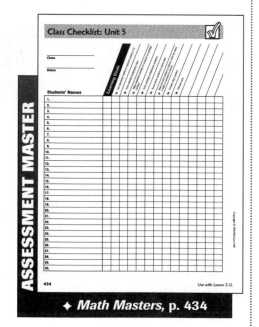

✦ *Math Masters*, p. 434

# Unit 6
# Assessment Overview

The main focus of this unit is whole-number division. The goal chart below shows ongoing assessment opportunities for observing students as they develop this skill. For example, to see how well students are progressing with Goal 6b, the chart shows that ongoing assessment opportunities related to this goal can be found in Lessons 6.1 and 6.2 on pages 370 and 375 of your *Teacher's Lesson Guide*. The chart on page 55 indicates where you can find slate and written problems to help you assess students' progress toward this same goal.

## Ongoing Assessment Opportunities

Ongoing assessment provides opportunities to observe students during regular interactions as they work independently and in groups. You can conduct ongoing assessment during teacher-guided instruction, Math Boxes sessions, mathematical mini-interviews, games, Mental Math and Reflexes sessions, strategy sharing, and slate work. The chart below provides a summary of ongoing assessment opportunities in Unit 6 as they relate to specific Unit 6 learning goals.

| | |
|---|---|
| **6a** **Beginning Goal** Identify locations on Earth for which latitude and longitude are given; find latitude and longitude for given locations. (Lessons 6.9 and 6.10) | Lesson 6.10, p. 415 |
| **6b** **Developing Goal** Solve whole-number division problems. (Lessons 6.1–6.3) | Lesson 6.1, p. 370<br>Lesson 6.2, p. 375 |
| **6e** **Developing Goal** Name and locate points specified by ordered number pairs on a coordinate grid. (Lessons 6.5 and 6.7) | Lesson 6.5, p. 389 |
| **6h** **Developing Goal** Use a circular protractor and a half-circle protractor to measure and draw angles. (Lessons 6.6–6.9) | Lesson 6.7, p. 400<br>Lesson 6.8, p. 405 |

# Product Assessment Opportunities

*Math Journals,* Math Boxes, Activity Sheets, *Math Masters,* math logs, and the results of Projects all provide product assessment opportunities. Here is an example of how you might use a rubric to assess a student's ability to write and solve multiplication and division number stories.

Lesson 6.11, p. 420

**ALTERNATIVE ASSESSMENT** **Write and Solve Multiplication and Division Number Stories**

This activity is intended to assess students' skills in writing multiplication and division number stories. Use your own rubric, or the sample rubric below, to evaluate students' work.

| Sample Rubric |
|---|
| **Beginning (B)**<br>The student writes a number story, but it is not connected to the concept of multiplication or division, displaying a lack of understanding for multiplication/division. A question and number model with a correct solution are missing. |
| **Developing (D)**<br>The student writes a number story that is connected appropriately to the concept of multiplication or division. The number model is written correctly, but the solution may be incorrect due to a simple error in computation or procedure. |
| **Secure (S)**<br>The student writes a number story that is connected to multiplication or division. It is evident that the student has a strong understanding of multiplication/division concepts. The student may write a multistep number story or one that has extra data included. A question and number model with a correct solution is given. |

# Periodic Assessment Opportunities

Here is a summary of the periodic assessment opportunities that are provided in Unit 6. Refer to Lesson 6.11 for details.

## Oral and Slate Assessment

In Lesson 6.11, you will find oral and slate assessment problems on pages 418 and 419.

## Written Assessment

In Lesson 6.11, you will find written assessment problems on page 419 (*Math Masters,* pp. 399–401).

See the chart on the next page to find oral, slate, and written assessment problems, as well as alternative assessment options that address specific learning goals.

| | | |
|---|---|---|
| **6a** | **Beginning Goal** Identify locations on Earth for which latitude and longitude are given; find latitude and longitude for given locations. (Lessons 6.9 and 6.10) | Slate Assessment, Problems 2 and 3 |
| **6b** | **Developing Goal** Solve whole-number division problems. (Lessons 6.1–6.3) | Written Assessment, Problems 8–10 Alternative Assessment Option |
| **6c** | **Developing Goal** Express the remainder of a whole-number division problem as a fraction and the answer as a mixed number. (Lessons 6.4 and 6.5) | Written Assessment, Problems 8 and 10 |
| **6d** | **Developing Goal** Interpret the remainder in division problems. (Lesson 6.4) | Written Assessment, Problems 12, 14, and 15 |
| **6e** | **Developing Goal** Name and locate points specified by ordered number pairs on a coordinate grid. (Lessons 6.5 and 6.7) | Written Assessment, Problem 11 |
| **6f** | **Developing Goal** Identify acute, right, obtuse, straight, and reflex angles. (Lesson 6.8) | Slate Assessment, Problem 1 Written Assessment, Problems 1–3 and 7 |
| **6g** | **Developing Goal** Make turns and fractions of turns; relate turns and angles. (Lessons 6.6 and 6.7) | Oral Assessment, Problems 1 and 2 |
| **6h** | **Developing Goal** Use a circular protractor and a half-circle protractor to measure and draw angles. (Lessons 6.6–6.9) | Written Assessment, Problems 1–6 Alternative Assessment Option |
| **6i** | **Developing Goal** Solve multiplication and division number stories. (Lessons 6.1 and 6.3) | Written Assessment, Problems 12–16 Alternative Assessment Option |

## Alternative Assessment

In Lesson 6.11, you will find alternative assessment options on page 420.

### ✦ Write and Solve Multiplication and Division Number Stories

Portfolio Ideas

To assess a student's skill at writing and solving multiplication and division number stories, use the rubric on page 54, or consider the following questions:

• Is the number story complete? (Is information given and a question posed?)

• Does the number story ask a question that can be answered using the information given?

• Does the number story reflect understanding of multiplication and division?

✦ *Math Masters*, p. 436

## ✦ Describe a Division Strategy

Develop a rubric similar to the rubric for multiplication on page 54, but tailor it to focus on division skills. Then use your rubric to assess a student's ability to describe a division strategy. Your rubric might include references to questions such as

- Does the student organize his or her work well?
- Does the student's strategy show a basic understanding of division; that is, does it include removing or dividing into equal groups?
- Does the student arrive at an accurate answer that the student can justify?

## ✦ Measure Angles with a Circular and Half-Circle Protractor

Students decide whether an angle was measured correctly. As you review a student's work, keep these questions in mind:

- Can the student see that there are two angles that can be measured, the smaller angle and the reflex angle?
- Does the student know which scale to use on a half-circle protractor?
- Can the student visually estimate the size of the smaller angle as less than 90° and thus know that Alexi's answer is incorrect?

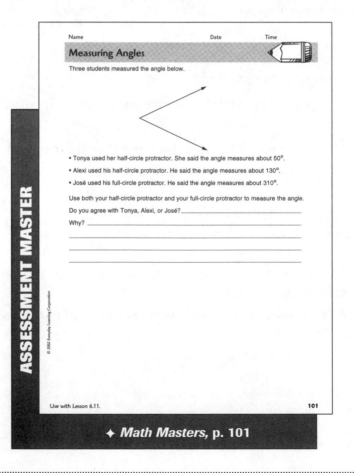

✦ *Math Masters,* p. 101

# Unit 7
# Assessment Overview

In this unit, students further develop their abilities to work with fractions. Depending on the specific skill, students' ability levels might range from Beginning to Secure. A good mix of ongoing assessment opportunities is suggested in the chart below for several learning goals that deal with fractions. Oral, written, and slate assessments for these same goals are listed in the chart on page 59.

## Ongoing Assessment Opportunities

Ongoing assessment provides opportunities to observe students during regular interactions as they work independently and in groups. You can conduct ongoing assessment during teacher-guided instruction, Math Boxes sessions, mathematical mini-interviews, games, Mental Math and Reflexes sessions, strategy sharing, and slate work. The chart below provides a summary of ongoing assessment opportunities in Unit 7 as they relate to specific Unit 7 learning goals.

| | |
|---|---|
| **7a** **Beginning Goal** Add and subtract fractions. (Lessons 7.4 and 7.5) | Lesson 7.4, p. 532 |
| **7e** **Developing Goal** Find equivalent fractions for given fractions. (Lessons 7.6 and 7.7) | Lesson 7.6, p. 543 <br> Lesson 7.7, p. 547 |
| **7f** **Secure Goal** Identify the whole for fractions. (Lessons 7.1, 7.3, and 7.10) | Lesson 7.1, p. 513 |
| **7h** **Secure Goal** Identify fractional parts of regions. (Lessons 7.1–7.3, 7.5, and 7.9) | Lesson 7.3, p. 526 |

## Product Assessment Opportunities

*Math Journals,* Math Boxes, Activity Sheets, *Math Masters,* math logs, and the results of Projects all provide product assessment opportunities. Here is an example of how you might use a rubric to assess a student's ability to describe a fraction addition or subtraction strategy.

Lesson 7.13, p. 580

ALTERNATIVE ASSESSMENT **Describe a Fraction Addition or Subtraction Strategy**

Most of your students should be able to use several methods to add and subtract fractions, but ability levels will vary. Some students will use manipulatives or draw models, whereas others may try to create their own pencil-and-paper algorithm. Use your own rubric, or the sample rubric below, to evaluate students' work.

Portfolio Ideas

### Sample Rubric

**Beginning (B)**
The student solves addition/subtraction fraction problems with like denominators, using pattern blocks or a clock face. Some assistance may be required. He or she is not able to use the same procedure and manipulative for problems with unlike denominators. The student is unable to articulate his or her strategy due to a lack of understanding of fractions and the procedure.

**Developing (D)**
The student solves addition/subtraction fraction problems with like and unlike denominators independently using pattern blocks or clock faces. He or she is able to describe the strategy used for like denominators but still struggles with writing about the strategy used for unlike denominators.

**Secure (S)**
The student solves addition/subtraction problems with like and unlike denominators independently. The student has moved beyond just using manipulatives and is also comfortable in drawing models or is beginning to develop a paper-pencil algorithm. It is evident that the student has an understating of fractions and the procedures used.

## Periodic Assessment Opportunities

Here is a summary of the periodic assessment opportunities that are provided in Unit 7. Refer to Lesson 7.13 for details.

### *Oral and Slate Assessment*

In Lesson 7.13, you will find oral and slate assessment problems on pages 577 and 578.

### *Written Assessment*

In Lesson 7.13, you will find written assessment problems on page 579 (*Math Masters,* pp. 402 and 403).

See the following chart to find oral, slate, and written assessment problems, as well as alternative assessment options that address specific learning goals.

| | | |
|---|---|---|
| **7a** | **Beginning Goal** Add and subtract fractions. (Lessons 7.4 and 7.5) | Slate Assessment, Problem 1<br>Written Assessment,<br>   Problem 16 |
| **7b** | **Developing Goal** Rename fractions with denominators of 10 and 100 as decimals. (Lesson 7.8) | Slate Assessment, Problem 2 |
| **7c** | **Developing Goal** Apply basic vocabulary and concepts associated with chance events. (Lesson 7.12) | Written Assessment,<br>   Problems 14 and 15 |
| **7d** | **Developing Goal** Compare and order fractions. (Lesson 7.9) | Oral Assessment, Problem 1<br>Written Assessment,<br>   Problems 5–10 |
| **7e** | **Developing Goal** Find equivalent fractions for given fractions. (Lessons 7.6 and 7.7) | Oral Assessment, Problem 2<br>Written Assessment,<br>   Problems 1–4 and 7 |
| **7f** | **Secure Goal** Identify the whole for fractions. (Lessons 7.1, 7.3, and 7.10) | Written Assessment,<br>   Problems 11–13 |
| **7g** | **Secure Goal** Identify fractional parts of a collection of objects. (Lesson 7.2) | Slate Assessment, Problem 3<br>Written Assessment,<br>   Problem 13 |
| **7h** | **Secure Goal** Identify fractional parts of regions. (Lessons 7.1–7.3, 7.5 and 7.9) | Slate Assessment, Problem 4<br>Written Assessment,<br>   Problems 11, 12, 14, and 16 |

## Alternative Assessment

In Lesson 7.13, you will find alternative assessment options on page 580.

### ✦ Describe a Fraction Addition or Subtraction Strategy

Students solve fraction addition and subtraction problems. They can solve the problems, using any method they choose. Encourage students to record their work. As you circulate, use a Class Checklist or Computer Grids to record students' progress. The rubric on page 58 can be used to evaluate students' work, or you can make your own.

### ✦ Collect Fraction Names

Students continue to find equivalent fractions in *Math Journal 2*, pages 356 and 357. They use the equivalent fractions rule to find equivalent fractions with denominators of 10 or 100 and then write the fractions as decimals. As you circulate to check students' work, keep these questions in mind:

• Can the student find more than one fraction equivalent to another?

• Does the student know how to use the equivalent fractions rule to find equivalent fractions?

• Does the student understand the relationship between fractions and decimals?

✦ *Math Masters*, p. 438

# Unit 8
# Assessment Overview

In this unit, students develop their skills at finding areas and perimeters. Students also are beginning to learn about scale drawings.

By this time, perhaps you have tried several different types of assessment strategies. Remember, as you use a balance of assessment approaches, the overall effectiveness of your assessment plan should improve. If there is still a major type of assessment, such as Ongoing, Product, or Periodic, that you haven't used, this unit might be a good time to try it.

## Ongoing Assessment Opportunities

Ongoing assessment provides opportunities to observe students during regular interactions as they work independently and in groups. You can conduct ongoing assessment during teacher-guided instruction, Math Boxes sessions, mathematical mini-interviews, games, Mental Math and Reflexes sessions, strategy sharing, and slate work. The chart below provides a summary of ongoing assessment opportunities in Unit 8 as they relate to specific Unit 8 learning goals.

| | | |
|---|---|---|
| **8a** | **Beginning Goal** Make and interpret scale drawings. (Lessons 8.2, 8.3, 8.5, and 8.6) | Lesson 8.3, p. 609 |
| **8b** | **Developing Goal** Use formulas to find areas of rectangles, parallelograms, and triangles. (Lessons 8.5–8.8) | Lesson 8.5, p. 620 <br> Lesson 8.7, p. 631 |
| **8c** | **Developing Goal** Find the perimeter of a polygon. (Lessons 8.1–8.3, 8.7, and 8.8) | Lesson 8.7, p. 631 |
| **8d** | **Developing/Secure Goal** Find the area of a figure by counting unit squares and fractions of unit squares inside the figure. (Lessons 8.3–8.8) | Lesson 8.3, p. 609 <br> Lesson 8.5, p. 620 |

# Product Assessment Opportunities

*Math Journals,* Math Boxes, Activity Sheets, *Math Masters,* math logs, and the results of Projects all provide product assessment opportunities. Here is an example of how you might use a rubric to assess a student's ability to find the area and perimeter of an irregular figure.

Lesson 8.9, p. 641

**ALTERNATIVE ASSESSMENT** Find the Area and Perimeter of an Irregular Figure

Most of your students should be able to divide the polygon into figures to find the area. Some students may use other ways to find the area. Use your own rubric, or the sample rubric below, to evaluate students' work.

Portfolio Ideas

### Sample Rubric

**Beginning (B)**
The student attempts to solve the problem, but assistance is required. He or she attempts to apply formulas by dividing the irregular polygon into rectangles but still counts some of the individual squares. It is evident that the student is not comfortable in using formulas for finding the area of rectangles, parallelograms, and triangles. The solution for area is incorrect, even though it is accurate in calculating the perimeter of the irregular polygon.

**Developing (D)**
The student solves the problem with little or no assistance. He or she is comfortable in dividing the irregular polygon into rectangles, parallelograms, and triangles. The answer may be incorrect due to neglecting to apply the formula for the area of triangles accurately or to a simple error in computation. The answer for finding the perimeter is correct.

**Secure (S)**
The student solves the problem with no assistance. It is evident that the student understands and applies the formulas for area of triangles, rectangles, and parallelograms. For example, the student may divide the irregular polygon into 1 large parallelogram (96 cm$^2$), 1 small triangle (6 cm$^2$), and 1 rectangle (24 cm$^2$). Correct answers for the area and perimeter of the irregular polygon are given.

# Periodic Assessment Opportunities

Here is a summary of the periodic assessment opportunities that are provided in Unit 8. Refer to Lesson 8.9 for details.

### Oral and Slate Assessment

In Lesson 8.9, you will find oral and slate assessment problems on pages 638 and 639.

### Written Assessment

In Lesson 8.9, you will find written assessment problems on pages 640 and 641 (*Math Masters,* pp. 404 and 405).

See the following chart to find oral, slate, and written assessment problems that address specific learning goals.

| | | |
|---|---|---|
| **8a** | **Beginning Goal** Make and interpret scale drawings. (Lessons 8.2, 8.3, and 8.5) | Slate Assessment, Problem 1 Written Assessment, Problems 8–11 |
| **8b** | **Developing Goal** Use formulas to find areas of rectangles, parallelograms, and triangles. (Lessons 8.5–8.8) | Oral Assessment, Problem 1 Written Assessment, Problems 3–7 |
| **8c** | **Developing Goal** Find the perimeter of a polygon. (Lessons 8.1, 8.2, and 8.7) | Oral Assessment, Problem 1 Written Assessment, Problems 1, 3–5, and 9 |
| **8d** | **Developing/Secure Goal** Find the area of a figure by counting unit squares and fractions of unit squares inside the figure. (Lessons 8.3–8.7) | Oral Assessment, Problem 1 Written Assessment, Problems 2 and 11 |

## Alternative Assessment

In Lesson 8.9, you will find alternative assessment options on pages 641 and 642.

### ✦ Find the Area and Perimeter of an Irregular Figure

Students use their own methods, other than counting squares, to find the area of an irregular polygon. Students are encouraged to divide the polygon into figures that enable them to use formulas to find the area. Use your own rubric or the rubric on page 61 to evaluate students' work.

### ✦ Make Enlargements

Students compare an original with an enlargement that is double in size. They find perimeters and areas and describe how the perimeter and area of the enlargement differ from that of the original. As you evaluate students' work, keep the following questions in mind:

• Does the student confuse perimeter and area?

• Can the student accurately find perimeter and area?

• Is the student able to see the relationship between perimeter and area of the enlargement and that of the original, or does the student presume that both are just doubled?

### ✦ Solve Perimeter and Area Problems

Students combine polygons to make a larger polygon. They then use the areas of the smaller polygons to find the area of the larger compound polygon. They also find perimeters. Keep the following questions in mind as you evaluate students' work:

• Can the student find areas and perimeters accurately?

• Does the student understand that he or she cannot combine perimeters of the smaller polygons to find the perimeter of the larger compound polygon?

---

**ASSESSMENT MASTER**

Class Checklist: Unit 8

Class

Dates

Students' Names

440     Use with Lesson 8.9.

**✦ Math Masters, p. 440**

# Unit 9
# Assessment Overview

By the time they complete Unit 9, students should be Secure in their abilities to give equivalencies between hundredth-fractions, decimals, and percents, and they should be developing their abilities to find these equivalencies for "easy" fractions. The chart on page 65 indicates where you can find written and slate assessments to measure students' progress toward these goals.

## Ongoing Assessment Opportunities

Ongoing assessment provides opportunities to observe students during regular interactions as they work independently and in groups. You can conduct ongoing assessment during teacher-guided instruction, Math Boxes sessions, mathematical mini-interviews, games, Mental Math and Reflexes sessions, strategy sharing, and slate work. The chart below provides a summary of ongoing assessment opportunities in Unit 9 as they relate to specific Unit 9 learning goals.

| | |
|---|---|
| **9a** **Beginning Goal** Use an estimation strategy to divide decimals by whole numbers. (Lesson 9.9) | Lesson 9.6, p. 690 |
| **9b** **Beginning Goal** Use an estimation strategy to multiply decimals by whole numbers. (Lesson 9.8) | Lesson 9.2, p. 665 |
| **9c** **Developing Goal** Find a percent or a fraction of a number. (Lessons 9.1–9.3 and 9.6) | Lesson 9.1, p. 659 |

## Product Assessment Opportunities

*Math Journals*, Math Boxes, Activity Sheets, *Math Masters*, math logs, and the results of Projects all provide product assessment opportunities. Here is an example of how you might use a rubric to assess a student's ability to find equivalent fractions and percents.

Lesson 9.10, p. 713

**ALTERNATIVE ASSESSMENT** **Find the "Fraction-of" and "Percent-of" a Design**

Most of your students should be able to color a design and find fractions and equivalent percentages for the colors. Use your own rubric, or the sample rubric on the next page, to evaluate students' work.

## Periodic Assessment Opportunities

Here is a summary of the periodic assessment opportunities that are provided in Unit 9. Refer to Lesson 9.10 for details.

### Oral and Slate Assessment

In Lesson 9.10, you will find oral and slate assessment problems on pages 711 and 712.

### Written Assessment

In Lesson 9.10, you will find written assessment problems on pages 712 and 713 (*Math Masters,* pp. 406–408).

See the following chart to find oral, slate, and written assessment problems, as well as alternative assessment options that address specific learning goals.

| | |
|---|---|
| **9a** **Beginning Goal** Use an estimation strategy to divide decimals by whole numbers. (Lesson 9.9) | Oral Assessment, Problem 1<br>Written Assessment,<br>  Problems 12–14<br>Alternative Assessment Option |
| **9b** **Beginning Goal** Use an estimation strategy to multiply decimals by whole numbers. (Lesson 9.8) | Oral Assessment, Problem 2<br>Written Assessment,<br>  Problems 9–11<br>Alternative Assessment Option |
| **9c** **Developing Goal** Find a percent or a fraction of a number. (Lessons 9.1–9.3 and 9.6) | Slate Assessment, Problem 1<br>Written Assessment,<br>  Problems 6–8<br>Alternative Assessment Option |
| **9d** **Developing Goal** Convert between "easy" fractions (fourths, fifths, and tenths), decimals, and percents. (Lessons 9.1–9.3) | Slate Assessment, Problem 2<br>Written Assessment,<br>  Problems 1, 3, and 6 |

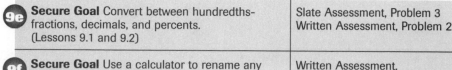

| | |
|---|---|
| **9e** **Secure Goal** Convert between hundredths-fractions, decimals, and percents. (Lessons 9.1 and 9.2) | Slate Assessment, Problem 3 Written Assessment, Problem 2 |
| **9f** **Secure Goal** Use a calculator to rename any fraction as a decimal or percent. (Lessons 9.3–9.5, and 9.7) | Written Assessment, Problems 4 and 5 |

## *Alternative Assessment*

In Lesson 9.10, you will find alternative assessment options on pages 713–715.

### ✦ Find the "Fraction-of" and "Percent-of" a Design

Students color a design and then find what fraction or percent of the total each color is. Students then write summary statements to describe their findings. Use the suggestions and rubric on pages 63 and 64 to evaluate students' work, or use the following questions:

• Are students able to write the correct fractions for their designs?

• Can students find equivalent percents for their fractions?

• Do students' percents add up to 100 percent?

### ✦ Describe a Decimal Division Strategy

Students solve a problem and then describe the strategy they used. As you circulate to check students' work, use a Class Checklist or Calendar Grids to record each student's progress. Keep the following questions in mind:

• Does the student organize his or her work well?

• Does the student show proficiency with whole-number division?

• Can the student estimate to place the decimal point in his or her answer?

• Can the student arrive at an accurate answer that he or she can justify?

### ✦ Describe a Decimal Multiplication Strategy

Students solve a problem and then describe the strategy they used. As you circulate to check students' work, use a Class Checklist or Calendar Grids to record each student's progress. Keep the following questions in mind:

• Does the student organize his or her work well?

• Does the student show proficiency with whole-number multiplication?

• Can the student estimate to place the decimal point in his or her answer?

• Can the student arrive at an accurate answer that he or she can justify?

✦ *Math Masters*, p. 442

# Unit 10
# Assessment Overview

The major topics of this unit are rotations, translations, reflections, and lines of symmetry. Depending on the specific skill, students' ability levels might range from Beginning to Secure. A good mix of ongoing assessment opportunities is suggested in the chart below for several learning goals that deal with fractions. Oral, written, and slate assessments for these same goals are listed in the chart on page 68.

## Ongoing Assessment Opportunities

Ongoing assessment provides opportunities to observe students during regular interactions as they work independently and in groups. You can conduct ongoing assessment during teacher-guided instruction, Math Boxes sessions, mathematical mini-interviews, games, Mental Math and Reflexes sessions, strategy sharing, and slate work. The chart below provides a summary of ongoing assessment opportunities in Unit 10 as they relate to specific Unit 10 learning goals.

| | | |
|---|---|---|
| **10a** | **Beginning Goal** Add integers. (Lesson 10.6) | Lesson 10.6, p. 760 |
| **10b** | **Beginning Goal** Rotate figures. (Lessons 10.4 and 10.5) | Lesson 10.5, p. 754 |
| **10c** | **Developing Goal** Translate figures. (Lesson 10.5) | Lesson 10.5, p. 754 |
| **10d** | **Secure Goal** Use a transparent mirror to draw the reflection of a figure. (Lessons 10.1–10.3 and 10.6) | Lesson 10.2, p. 737 |

## Product Assessment Opportunities

*Math Journals,* Math Boxes, Activity Sheets, *Math Masters,* math logs, and the results of Projects all provide product assessment opportunities. On the next page is an example of how you might use a rubric to assess a student's ability to create frieze patterns.

## ENRICHMENT  Creating Frieze Patterns

Students make frieze patterns by following the directions in *Math Masters,* page 163. Students present their completed patterns to the class and describe any reflections, translations or rotations used. Use your own rubric, or the sample rubric below, to evaluate students' work.

**Portfolio Ideas**

### Sample Rubric

**Beginning (B)**
The student creates a template by drawing and cutting a simple design on a 3-inch by 3-inch square. The student has difficulty using the template to create a frieze pattern. As a result, the student is unable to describe any reflections, translations, or rotations used in the pattern.

**Developing (D)**
The student creates a template by drawing and cutting a simple design on a 3-inch by 3-inch square. The student creates frieze patterns, using the template that involves translations, reflections, or rotations, but typically not a combination. The student describes his or her pattern by applying the terminology of reflections, translations, or rotations appropriately.

**Secure (S)**
The student creates a template by drawing a simple design on a 3-inch by 3-inch square. Some students at this level may create a more elaborate design. Using the template, the student creates a frieze pattern that involves a combination of translations, reflections, and rotations. The student describes his or her pattern by applying the appropriate terminology and understanding of concepts.

## Periodic Assessment Opportunities

Here is a summary of the periodic assessment opportunities that are provided in Unit 10. Refer to Lesson 10.7 for details.

### Oral and Slate Assessment

In Lesson 10.7, you will find oral and slate assessment problems on pages 764 and 765.

### Written Assessment

In Lesson 10.7, you will find written assessment problems on page 765 (*Math Masters,* pp. 409 and 410).

See the following chart to find oral, slate, and written assessment problems, as well as alternative assessment options that address specific learning goals.

| | |
|---|---|
| **10a** **Beginning Goal** Add integers. (Lesson 10.6) | Slate Assessment, Problem 1 Written Assessment, Problem 10 |
| **10b** **Beginning Goal** Rotate figures. (Lessons 10.4 and 10.5) | Oral Assessment, Problem 1 Written Assessment, Problem 7 |
| **10c** **Developing Goal** Translate figures. (Lesson 10.5) | Written Assessment, Problem 6 |

| | | |
|---|---|---|
| 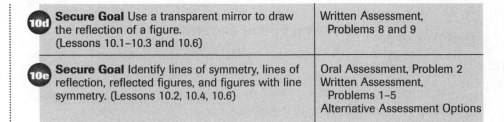 **Secure Goal** Use a transparent mirror to draw the reflection of a figure. (Lessons 10.1–10.3 and 10.6) | Written Assessment, Problems 8 and 9 | |
| **10e** **Secure Goal** Identify lines of symmetry, lines of reflection, reflected figures, and figures with line symmetry. (Lessons 10.2, 10.4, 10.6) | Oral Assessment, Problem 2 Written Assessment, Problems 1–5 Alternative Assessment Options | |

## Alternative Assessment

In Lesson 10.7, you will find alternative assessment options on pages 766 and 767.

### ✦ Create Reflections with Pattern Blocks or Centimeter Cubes

Each partner uses pattern blocks or centimeter cubes to draw a pattern and then trades patterns with his or her partner. Each partner reflects the pattern over a fold in the paper that acts as a line of symmetry. As you circulate to check students' work, keep these questions in mind:

• Does the student reflect the pattern along the fold in the paper?

• Does the student's final drawing show a reflection?

### ✦ Interpret a Cartoon

Students draw and interpret lines of symmetry in a cartoon. Circulate to assess students' understanding. You might keep these questions in mind:

• Is the student able to interpret the cartoon? In other words, does he or she understand that Ruthie is talking about line symmetry and not fractions?

• Does the student draw examples of line symmetry in the figure "8" correctly? In other words, "up and down" symmetry creates a three, and a line drawn across the "8" produces two zeros.

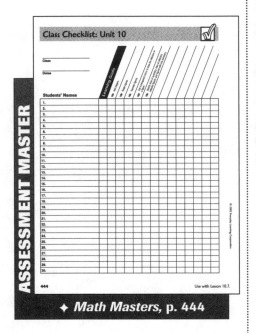

✦ *Math Masters, p. 444*

# Unit 11
# Assessment Overview

As you near the end of the Fourth-Grade *Everyday Mathematics* program, reflect on your success in developing a balanced assessment plan. Think about which assessment strategies worked best. Are there strategies that you did not have time to try this year, but that you would like to try next year? To help you remember them next fall, record your thoughts on the note pages in this book.

## Ongoing Assessment Opportunities

Ongoing assessment provides opportunities to observe students during regular interactions as they work independently and in groups. You can conduct ongoing assessment during teacher-guided instruction, Math Boxes sessions, mathematical mini-interviews, games, Mental Math and Reflexes sessions, strategy sharing, and slate work. The chart below provides a summary of ongoing assessment opportunities in Unit 11 as they relate to specific Unit 11 learning goals.

| | |
|---|---|
| **11a** **Beginning Goal** Use a formula to calculate volumes of rectangular prisms. (Lesson 11.5) | Lesson 11.5, p. 809 |
| **11c** **Developing Goal** Add positive and negative integers. (Lesson 11.6) | Lesson 11.3, p. 798 <br> Lesson 11.5, p. 811 |
| **11d** **Developing Goal** Estimate the weight of objects in ounces or grams; weigh objects in ounces or grams. (Lesson 11.1) | Lesson 11.1, p. 784 <br> Lesson 11.6, p. 817 |
| **11e** **Developing Goal** Solve cube-stacking volume problems. (Lessons 11.4 and 11.5) | Lesson 11.5, p. 809 |
| **11f** **Developing Goal** Describe properties of geometric solids. (Lessons 11.2 and 11.3) | Lesson 11.2, p. 790 |

## Product Assessment Opportunities

*Math Journals,* Math Boxes, Activity Sheets, *Math Masters,* math logs, and the results of Projects all provide product assessment opportunities. On the next page is an example of how you might use a rubric to assess a student's ability to solve a multi-step volume problem.

**ALTERNATIVE ASSESSMENT** Solve a Record Rainfall Problem

Some of your students should be able to solve this problem with little or no direction, but many might need some help with getting started. Use your own rubric, or the sample rubric below, to evaluate students' work.

### Sample Rubric

**Beginning (B)**
The students require teacher assistance in order to attempt the problem. The group experiences difficulties calculating the area of the classroom, which may be inaccurate due to a measurement error. Converting 42 inches to 3.5 feet may also pose difficulties, with each suggested strategy requiring teacher guidance. The answers are incorrect or unreasonable due to inaccurate measurements, conversions, or computational errors. The written explanations are unclear due to a lack of understanding of the strategies and concepts utilized.

**Developing (D)**
The students attempt to solve the problem with little or no teacher assistance. The group calculates the area of the classroom but may need help to convert inches of rain to feet. The group calculates a reasonable volume of rainwater for the classroom, along with an approximate weight of the water in pounds, but needs a suggested strategy on how to convert the pounds into approximate tons. The written explanation articulates a partial understanding of the strategy and the mathematics used to solve the problem. Some valuable information is missing; for example, why 42 inches is converted to feet.

**Secure (S)**
The students attempt to solve the problem without teacher assistance. The group works through the problem, experiencing little or no difficulty. Solutions are reasonable and the written explanations articulate a clear understanding of the strategies used and the mathematics applied in order to solve the problem.

## Periodic Assessment Opportunities

Here is a summary of the periodic assessment opportunities that are provided in Unit 11. Refer to Lesson 11.8 for details.

### *Oral and Slate Assessment*

In Lesson 11.8, you will find oral and slate assessment problems on pages 826 and 827.

### *Written Assessment*

In Lesson 11.8, you will find written assessment problems on pages 827 and 828 (*Math Masters,* pp. 411 and 412).

See the following chart to find oral, slate, and written assessment problems that address specific learning goals.

| | | |
|---|---|---|
| **11a** **Beginning Goal** Use a formula to calculate volumes of rectangular prisms. (Lesson 11.5) | Written Assessment, Problem 7 |
| **11b** **Beginning Goal** Subtract positive and negative integers. (Lesson 11.6) | Slate Assessment, Problem 1<br>Written Assessment, Problem 9 |
| **11c** **Developing Goal** Add positive and negative integers. (Lesson 11.6) | Slate Assessment, Problem 1<br>Written Assessment, Problem 8 |
| **11d** **Developing Goal** Estimate the weight of objects in ounces or grams; weigh objects in ounces or grams. (Lesson 11.1) | Oral Assessment, Problem 1<br>Written Assessment,<br>  Problem 10 |
| **11e** **Developing Goal** Solve cube-stacking volume problems. (Lessons 11.4 and 11.5) | Oral Assessment, Problem 2<br>Written Assessment, Problem 6 |
| **11f** **Developing Goal** Describe properties of geometric solids. (Lessons 11.2 and 11.3) | Written Assessment,<br>  Problems 1–5 |

## Alternative Assessment

In Lesson 11.8, you will find alternative assessment options on page 828.

### ✦ Solve a Record Rainfall Problem

Use *Math Masters,* p. 189, to assess students' abilities to find the volume of a rectangular solid and convert between inches and feet. Students work in small groups to solve the problem. You may want to use the rubric on page 70 to help evaluate students' work. As you circulate around the classroom to observe group work, keep the following questions in mind:

• Has the group been able to find the area of the classroom floor?

• Did they see the need to convert 42 inches to feet? If so, were they able to do so?

• Were they able to find the volume 42 inches of water would fill in their classroom?

• Could they find the weight of the water?

✦ *Math Masters,* p. 446

# Unit 12
# Assessment Overview

Looking back over the Fourth-Grade *Everyday Mathematics* program, have you been able to establish a balance of Ongoing, Product, and Periodic Assessment strategies? Have your strategies included keeping anecdotal records based on observations of students' progress, as well as the use of written assessments? This might be a good time to evaluate your assessment strategies and think of what approaches you might consider for next year.

## Ongoing Assessment Opportunities

Ongoing assessment provides opportunities to observe students during regular interactions as they work independently and in groups. You can conduct ongoing assessment during teacher-guided instruction, Math Boxes sessions, mathematical mini-interviews, games, Mental Math and Reflexes sessions, strategy sharing, and slate work. The chart below provides a summary of ongoing assessment opportunities in Unit 12 as they relate to specific Unit 12 learning goals.

| | |
|---|---|
| **12c** **Developing Goal** Evaluate reasonableness of rate data. (Lessons 12.3 and 12.6) | Lesson 12.6, p. 872 |
| **12e** **Secure Goal** Use rate tables, if necessary, to solve rate problems. (Lessons 12.2–12.4 and 12.6) | Lesson 12.2, p. 851 Lesson 12.6, p. 872 |

## Product Assessment Opportunities

*Math Journals,* Math Boxes, Activity Sheets, *Math Masters,* math logs, and the results of Projects all provide product assessment opportunities. On the next page is an example of how you might use a rubric to assess a student's ability to work rate problems.

**ALTERNATIVE ASSESSMENT** Solve Multi-Step Problems
Involving Rates

Most of your students should be able to use several
methods for solving these problems, but ability levels will
vary. Some students will use a combination of strategies
while others will rely on just one. Use your own rubric, or
the sample rubric below, to evaluate students' work.

Portfolio
Ideas

### Sample Rubric

**Beginning (B)**
The group solves Part A of the problem with some teacher assistance needed. Without
assistance, this group may answer 1 package (3 * 15 = 45), not considering the given data that
each person needs 5 cookies. The written explanation displays some lack of understanding of
rates. (See page 114 in the *Teacher's Lesson Guide* for suggestions.)

For Part B, the group selects 4 packages of cookies that simply have the lowest price, ignoring
the weight of the packages and the price per ounce. The group also ignores the requirement of
3 pounds of cookies needed. Questions 3 and 4 may be answered correctly, but need guidance
in calculating cost per ounce. The written explanation reflects a lack of understanding of the
problem and application of rate concepts.

**Developing (D)**
The group of students solves Part A without teacher assistance. They work through the problem
using a solution strategy that displays an understanding of rates (See page 114 of the *Teacher's
Lesson Guide* for examples of strategies.)

For Part B, the group begins to work on the problem but may need guidance or suggestions to
get started. Once given a suggestion, the group works through the problem. (See page 114 and
115 of the *Teacher's Lesson Guide* for possible suggestions.) Using one or a combination of
strategies, the group articulates in writing an understanding of how they solved the problem.

**Secure (S)**
The group of students solves both parts of the problem without teacher assistance. The group
uses a combination of strategies to solve Part B and is able to write a clear explanation to
display a Secure understanding of the problem and application of rate concepts.

## Periodic Assessment Opportunities

Here is a summary of the periodic assessment opportunities that
are provided in Unit 12. Refer to Lesson 12.7 for details.

### *Oral and Slate Assessment*

In Lesson 12.7, you will find oral and slate assessment problems on
pages 875 and 876.

### *Written Assessment*

In Lesson 12.7, you will find written assessment problems on
page 877 (*Math Masters,* pages 413 and 414).

See the following chart to find oral, slate, and written assessment
problems, as well as alternative assessment options that address
specific learning goals.

| | | |
|---|---|---|
| **12a** **Developing Goal** Find unit rates. (Lessons 12.4 and 12.5) | Slate Assessment, Problems 1 and 2 Written Assessment, Problem 2a Alternative Assessment Option |
| **12b** **Developing Goal** Calculate unit prices to determine which product is the "better buy." (Lessons 12.4 and 12.5) | Written Assessment, Problems 4 and 5 Alternative Assessment Option |
| **12c** **Developing Goal** Evaluate reasonableness of rate data. (Lessons 12.3 and 12.6) | Oral Assessment, Problem 1 Written Assessment, Problem 1 |
| **12d** **Developing Goal** Collect and compare rate data. (Lessons 12.1, 12.3, and 12.5) | Written Assessment, Problems 4 and 5 |
| **12e** **Secure Goal** Use rate tables, if necessary, to solve rate problems. (Lessons 12.2–12.4 and 12.6) | Slate Assessment, Problems 1 and 2 Written Assessment, Problems 2b, 3, and 6 |

## Alternative Assessment

In Lesson 12.7, you will find an alternative assessment option on pages 877 and 878.

### ✦ Solve Multi-Step Problems Involving Rates

Students work in small groups to solve a set of multi-step rate problems. Use the rubric on page 73 to evaluate students' understanding. Or, as you circulate around the classroom to observe group work, keep the following questions in mind:

- Is the group able to approach each problem step by step in an organized fashion?
- Was the group able to find unit rates when they needed them?
- Does the group have a strategy that it can justify for solving each problem?
- Did the group arrive at the correct answers?

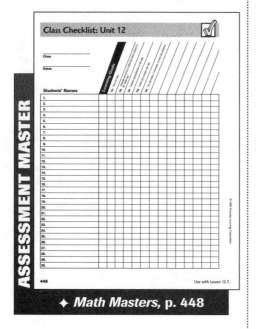

# Assessment Masters

# How to Use the Masters

NOTE: This page provides a brief summary of how the general Assessment Masters may be used. The uses of these masters are described in more detail near the front of this book on pages 3–32.

The *Assessment Handbook* contains reduced versions of all of the Assessment Masters found in your *Math Masters* book. You can use these reduced pages to assist you in developing your assessment plan. The following general masters may be adapted to suit your needs; however, the suggestions below may be helpful.

Use the **List of Assessment Sources** to keep track of the sources that you are currently using. As you plan your assessment, aim for the balance of techniques that will meet your students' needs.

On the **Individual Profile of Progress**

• Copy the Learning Goals from the Review and Assessment Lesson at the end of each unit. (See the *Teacher's Lesson Guide.*)

• Make as many copies of the form as you need for each student in your class.

• Keep track of each student's progress on each unit's skills and concepts using this form.

• Check whether each student is Beginning, Developing, or Secure in each of the content areas.

• You may alternatively wish to use the **Class Checklist.**

Make several copies of the **Class Progress Indicator.** Use one page for each mathematical topic being assessed. Fill in the topic you wish to assess under the chart heading, and then write each student's name in the appropriate box, indicating whether he or she is Beginning, Developing, or Secure.

All of the other forms are to be passed out to students. Use the **Interest Inventories** to find out how children feel about mathematics. Their frank responses can be a useful planning tool for you. The **math log** forms can also provide insight into how comfortable students feel with the math content and, therefore, may also be useful planning tools. There are three versions of math logs provided: a Weekly Math Log, a generic all-purpose Math Log, and a more specific Number-Story Math Log. Both **Self-Assessment** forms should be used as attachments to portfolio items. After students have chosen the work they wish to include in their portfolios, have them reflect on their choices, using these forms.

Assessment Masters

---

**Name**    **Date**    **Time**

## Unit 1 Checking Progress

**1.** Part of each polygon below is hidden. One of the 3 polygons is a **parallelogram,** another is a **trapezoid,** and another is a regular **hexagon.** Write the correct name of each polygon on the line.

trapezoid      parallelogram      hexagon

**2.**

A   B   C   D   E   F

**a.** Which of the above shapes are not polygons? __B, C, F__

**b.** Choose one of the shapes that is not a polygon. Tell why it is not a polygon.

**Sample answers: B has two sides that cross; C has curved sides; the sides of F do not form a closed path.**

© 2002 Everyday Learning Corporation

Use with Lesson 1.9.

387

---

**Name**    **Date**    **Time**

## Unit 1 Checking Progress (cont.)

**3.** I am a quadrangle.
I have 4 right angles.
I am not a square.

**a.** What am I? __rectangle__

**b.** Draw a picture of me in the space at the right.

**Sample answer:**

**c.** Use the letters A, B, C, and D to label the vertices of the quadrangle you drew.

**d.** Name the quadrangle in four different ways.

ABCD   BCDA   Or reverse order: DCBA,
CDAB   DABC   ADCB, and so on.

**4.** Draw $\overline{AB}$ parallel to $\overleftrightarrow{CD}$. Draw line $\overleftrightarrow{EF}$ so that it intersects line segment AB and ray CD.

For Problems 5–8, fill in the ovals below to show your answers. There is more than one correct answer for some items, so you may need to fill in more than one oval.

**5.** ○ $\overrightarrow{OP}$  **6.** ○ $\overline{LA}$
● $\overleftrightarrow{OP}$    ○ $\overrightarrow{AL}$
● $\overrightarrow{PO}$    ● $\overrightarrow{LA}$

**7.** ● quadrangle  **8.** ○ square
● polygon    ● rhombus
● parallelogram    ○ trapezoid

© 2002 Everyday Learning Corporation

Use with Lesson 1.9.

388

---

Assessment Masters    **77**

## Unit 2 Checking Progress

Name _____ Date _____ Time _____

1. Su Lin wanted to show the number 27 on her calculator. The 7-key on her calculator was broken, so this is what she did:

   3 ⊠ 8 ⊞ 3 Enter 27

   Find two other ways to show 27 without using the 7-key.
   Try to use different numbers and operations. **Sample answers:**

   a. 30 ⊟ 3 Enter

   b. 5 ⊠ 10 ⊟ 23 Enter

Add or subtract.

2. $129 + 462 =$ **591**

3. $507 + 1,829 =$ **2,336**

4. **7,300** $= 4,326 + 2,974$

5. $208 - 72 =$ **136**

6. **276** $= 924 - 648$

7. **1,868** $= 4,361 - 2,493$

Use with Lesson 2.10.

390

---

## Unit 1 Checking Progress (cont.)

Name _____ Date _____ Time _____

9. a. Sketch each figure in the third column of the table.

| Label | Geometric Figure | Sketch |
| --- | --- | --- |
| A | rhombus | |
| B | parallel line segments | |
| C | right angle | |
| D | trapezoid | |
| E | hexagon | |
| F | triangle | |

b. Use your Geometry Template and straightedge to draw one picture of yourself doing something you like to do. Include as many geometric figures listed in the table as you can. Label each figure in your picture with its letter from the table. Draw your picture in the space below or on the back of this page.

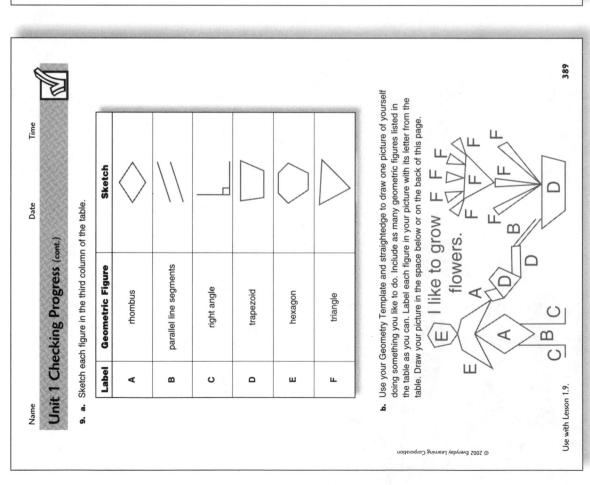

I like to grow flowers.

Use with Lesson 1.9.

389

Name     Date     Time

## Unit 3 Checking Progress

© 2002 Everyday Learning Corporation

Fill in the missing number in each Fact Triangle.

1. Triangle: 35, *, /, 5, 7

2. Triangle: 16, *, /, 4, 4

3. Triangle: 72, *, /, 8, 9

Next to each of the following, write "T" if it is true, "F" if it is false, or "?" if you can't tell.

4. $6 * 8 = 48$   __T__

5. $9 * 6$   __?__

6. $3 * 3 = 45 / 5$   __T__

7. $4 * 6 < 30$   __T__

8. $3 * (4 + 5) = 17$   __F__

9. $(7 * 4) / 2 > 3 * 7$   __F__

Make a true sentence by filling in the missing number.

10. __85__ $= (8 * 9) + 13$

11. __35__ $= (12 - 5) * 5$

12. $(14 - 6) + (32 / 8) =$ __12__

13. $(12 / 4) * (24 / 4) =$ __18__

Make a true sentence by inserting parentheses.

14. $30 - (15 + 2) = 13$

15. $56 / (8 + 48) = 1$

16. $26 - (3 + 13) = 10$

17. $(6 * 4) + 57 = 81$

Find the solution of each open sentence.

18. $19 = 12 + x$   Solution: __7__

19. $4 * n = 16$   Solution: __4__

20. $z / 3 = 6$   Solution: __18__

21. $x / 6 = 5$   Solution: __30__

22. $17 - x = 8$   Solution: __9__

23. $4 * 5 = 30 - t$   Solution: __10__

392

Use with Lesson 3.12.

---

Name     Date     Time

## Unit 2 Checking Progress (cont.)

Ivan asked his classmates to estimate the number of cans of soda they drink each week. He recorded the information on the tally chart below. Use Ivan's tally chart to answer the following questions:

| Number of Cans of Soda | Number of Students |
| --- | --- |
| 0 | /// |
| 1 | // |
| 2 | ₩₩ |
| 3 | ₩₩ / |
| 4 | /// |
| 5 | // |
| 6 |  |
| 7 | / |
| 8 | / |

8. What is the maximum number of cans? __8__

9. What is the minimum number of cans? __0__

10. What is the range of the number of cans? __8__

11. What is the mode of the number of cans? __3__

12. What is the median number of cans? __3__

13. Explain how you found the median. Sample answer: When the data are listed in order, the two middle numbers are both 3.

14. Make a bar graph of the data.

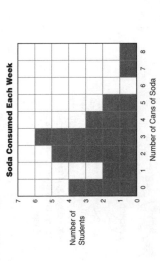

Soda Consumed Each Week

391

© 2002 Everyday Learning Corporation

Use with Lesson 2.10.

Name                                  Date                              Time

## Unit 3 Checking Progress (cont.)

Solve the following addition and subtraction number stories:

24. The Golden Gate Bridge was completed in 1937. The length of its main span is 4,200 feet. The San Francisco Bay Bridge was completed in 1936. The length of its main span is 2,310 feet. How much longer is the Golden Gate Bridge than the San Francisco Bay Bridge?

_1,890_ feet

25. A European eel can live up to 88 years. A giant tortoise can live about 62 years longer. How long can a giant tortoise live?

About _150_ years

26. India is the top movie-producing country in the world. In one year it produced 754 movies. That year, the United States came in second with 685 movies. In all, how many movies did these two countries produce that year?

_1,439_ movies

27. a. The largest book store chain in the United States has 950 stores. Suppose they add 65 new stores. How many stores will they have then?

_1,015_ stores

b. Suppose that instead of opening stores, they close 85 stores. How many stores will they have then?

_865_ stores

Use with Lesson 3.12.

---

Name                                  Date                              Time

## Unit 3 Checking Progress (cont.)

Use the map and map scale to answer the following questions:

Lodwar
Moyale
Wajir
KENYA
△ Mount Kenya
⊕ Nairobi
Mombasa

0  100  200 mi
1 inch represents 200 miles

28. The distance between Mombasa and Wajir is about _2_ inches on the map. That is about _400_ miles.

29. The distance between Nairobi and Lodwar is about _1$\frac{1}{2}$_ inches on the map. That is about _300_ miles.

Use with Lesson 3.12.

Name     Date     Time

## Unit 4 Checking Progress

1. Write 2 numbers between 0 and 1. Use decimals.    0.5, 0.73
2. Write 2 numbers between 2 and 3. Use decimals.    2.1, 2.555

Sample answers.

Circle the best answer.

3. The length of my foot is about    1.85 cm    (18.5 cm)    185 cm
4. A child's height is about    (1.25 m)    12.5 m    125 m
5. The cost of 12 pieces of gum at a nickel a piece is    $0.06    ($0.60)    $6.00
6. The number for the point marked X on the number line is    0.05    (0.5)    1.5

0   X   1

7. Use your ruler to measure the line segment below to the nearest centimeter.

10 cm

Use your ruler to measure the line segments below to the nearest millimeter.
Record your measurements in millimeters and centimeters.

8. A    B    82 mm    8.2 cm
9. C    D    58 mm    5.8 cm
10. Draw a line segment that is 12.5 centimeters long.
11. Draw a line segment that is 45 millimeters long.

Use with Lesson 4.11.

---

Name     Date     Time

## Unit 4 Checking Progress (cont.)

Write < or > to make a true number sentence.

12. 5.46 $<$ 5.9
13. 7.003 $>$ 3.7
14. 4.8 + 6.9 $>$ 3.4 + 7.7
15. 3.85 − 3.46 $<$ 9.1 − 6.2

16. Write the following set of numbers in order from smallest to largest.
0.001, 4.3, 4.05, 0.6, 0.06, 0.1    0.001, 0.06, 0.1, 0.6, 4.05, 4.3

Complete.

17. 2 m = 200 cm
18. 1.46 m = 146 cm
19. 36 mm = 3.6 cm
20. 120 mm = 12 cm

21. The winner of the women's 400-meter run in the 1972 Olympics ran the race in about 51.08 seconds. The winning time in the 1996 Olympics was 48.25 seconds—an Olympic record. How much faster was the winning time in 1996 than in 1972?

Answer: 2.83 seconds

Number model: 51.08 − 48.25 = 2.83

22. Mrs. Austin had $98.37 in her savings account. She withdrew $42.50. A week later, she deposited $38.25. What is the new balance in her savings account?

Answer: $94.12

Write what you did to find the answer.

Sample answer: First I subtracted $42.50 from $98.37 and got a difference of $55.87. Then I added $38.25 to $55.87 and got the new balance of $94.12.

Use with Lesson 4.11.

Name                                    Date                    Time

## Unit 5 Checking Progress

1. Which of the following is closest to the sum of 486 and 732?

   800    1,000    (1,200)    1,400

2. Which of the following is closest to the product of 58 and 34?

   180    (1,800)    18,000    180,000

An average of about 10,000 babies are born in the United States each day.

3. About how many babies are born in a week?  70,000

4. About how many babies are born in a month?  range: 280,000 to 310,000

5. Are there more or less than a million babies born in the U.S. in a year?  more

According to the 1990 U.S. Census, the population of Texas was 16,986,510.

6. Round this number to the nearest million.  17,000,000

7. Round it to the nearest thousand.  16,987,000

8. In Texas, there are about 700 registered motor vehicles for every 1,000 people. Which of the following is the best estimate for the number of registered motor vehicles in Texas?

   (12 million)    11,891,000    11,890,557

   Explain why you chose this answer.  Sample answer: Population (16,986,510) and registered vehicles (700 per 1,000) are not exact. So an answer rounded to millions is accurate enough.

Write > or <.

9. $10,000,000 > 7,508,976$

10. $368,972 > 364,986$

11. $9 \text{ trillion} > 54,000,000,000$

12. $746,390,299 > 10^6$

© 2002 Everyday Learning Corporation

Name                                    Date                    Time

## Unit 5 Checking Progress (cont.)

Multiply.

13. $8 * 6 = 48$

    $80 * 6 = 480$

    $8 * 600 = 4,800$

14. $3 * 7 = 21$

    $30 * 70 = 2,100$

    $300 * 70 = 21,000$

Multiply. Show your work.

15. $8 * 67 = 536$

16. $43 * 6 = 258$

17. $74 * 53 = 3,922$

18. $23 * 19 = 437$

19. Mrs. Green wants to buy a washing machine and pay for it in 1 year. L-Mart offers two plans and she wants to choose the cheaper one.

    Plan A: $7 each week; a total of 52 payments.

    Plan B: $27 each month; a total of 12 payments.

    Which plan should Mrs. Green choose?  Plan B

    Explain how you made your choice.  Plan A would cost $364 (7 * 52), while Plan B would cost $324 (12 * 27).

Name    Date    Time

## Unit 6 Checking Progress (cont.)

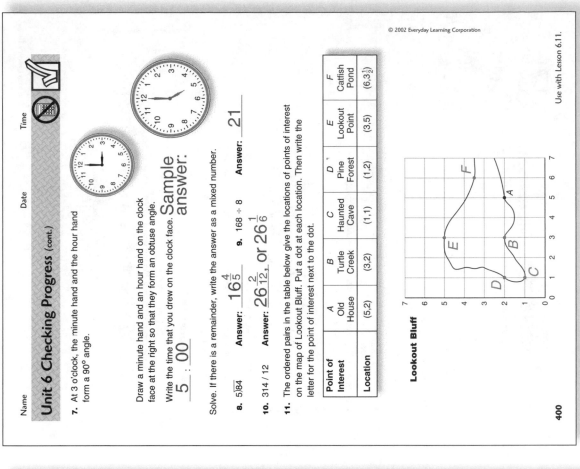

7. At 3 o'clock, the minute hand and the hour hand form a 90° angle.

Draw a minute hand and an hour hand on the clock face at the right so that they form an obtuse angle. Sample answer:

Write the time that you drew on the clock face.

5 : 00

Solve. If there is a remainder, write the answer as a mixed number.

8. 5)‾84‾    Answer: $16\frac{4}{5}$    9. 168 ÷ 8    Answer: 21

10. 314 / 12    Answer: $26\frac{2}{12}$, or $26\frac{1}{6}$

11. The ordered pairs in the table below give the locations of points of interest on the map of Lookout Bluff. Put a dot at each location. Then write the letter for the point of interest next to the dot.

| Point of Interest | A Old House | B Turtle Creek | C Haunted Cave | D Pine Forest | E Lookout Point | F Catfish Pond |
|---|---|---|---|---|---|---|
| Location | (5,2) | (3,2) | (1,1) | (1,2) | (3,5) | $(6,3\frac{1}{2})$ |

**Lookout Bluff**

Use with Lesson 6.11.

400

---

Name    Date    Time

## Unit 6 Checking Progress

Measure each angle below as accurately as you can. For each angle, circle the type: acute, right, obtuse, straight, or reflex.

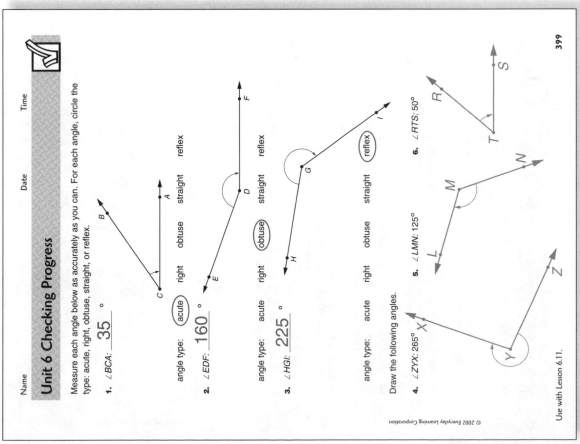

1. ∠BCA: 35 °

angle type: (acute)   right   obtuse   straight   reflex

2. ∠EDF: 160 °

angle type: acute   right   (obtuse)   straight   reflex

3. ∠HGI: 225 °

angle type: acute   right   obtuse   straight   (reflex)

Draw the following angles.

4. ∠ZYX: 265°

5. ∠LMN: 125°

6. ∠RTS: 50°

Use with Lesson 6.11.

399

## Unit 6 Checking Progress (cont.)

Name      Date      Time

Solve these multiplication and division number stories.

12. A jumbo box of Ginger Man Cookies contains 38 cookies. Tina and her two sisters decide to share them equally. How many whole cookies will each girl get?

    **12** cookies

13. When it snows, DeShawn charges $2 for every sidewalk he shovels and $3 for every driveway he shovels. If he shovels 6 sidewalks and 3 driveways, how much does he earn?

    $ **21**

14. Grace baked 76 muffins for the fourth grade breakfast party and put them on plates. Each plate holds 8 muffins. How many plates were needed to hold all of the muffins?

    **10** plates

15. Dugan and his 3 friends went to the video store. They rented several movies and bought snacks to eat while watching them. The total cost was $21.00. The friends split the bill evenly. How much did each person pay?

    $ **5.25**

16. Jennifer is saving up for basketball camp. If she puts $20 in the bank each week, how much will she have saved after 20 weeks?

    $ **400**

Use with Lesson 6.11.

401

---

## Unit 7 Checking Progress

Name      Date      Time

For each fraction, write two equivalent fractions. **Sample answers:**

1. $\frac{1}{2}$   $\frac{5}{10}$   $\frac{7}{14}$     2. $\frac{1}{3}$   $\frac{3}{9}$   $\frac{10}{30}$

3. $\frac{2}{5}$   $\frac{4}{10}$   $\frac{20}{50}$     4. $\frac{6}{8}$   $\frac{3}{4}$   $\frac{12}{16}$

Write >, <, or = between each pair of fractions.

5. $\frac{5}{6}$ > $\frac{5}{8}$      6. $\frac{11}{12}$ > $\frac{5}{12}$

7. $\frac{2}{3}$ = $\frac{8}{12}$      8. $\frac{2}{7}$ < $\frac{9}{10}$

Write each set of fractions in order from smallest to largest.

9. $\frac{1}{7}, \frac{1}{2}, \frac{1}{5}, \frac{1}{10}, \frac{1}{3}$    $\frac{1}{10}$ $\frac{1}{7}$ $\frac{1}{5}$ $\frac{1}{3}$ $\frac{1}{2}$

10. $\frac{2}{10}, \frac{9}{10}, \frac{7}{10}, \frac{1}{10}, \frac{5}{10}$    $\frac{1}{10}$ $\frac{2}{10}$ $\frac{5}{10}$ $\frac{7}{10}$ $\frac{9}{10}$

Use your pattern blocks to help you solve Problems 11 and 12.

11. Look at the "whole" box to the right.

Whole

a. If the red trapezoid is the whole, what fraction of the whole is

     1 green triangle? $\frac{1}{3}$      1 blue rhombus? $\frac{2}{3}$

b. What fraction of the red trapezoid do

     1 green triangle and 1 blue rhombus cover? $\frac{1}{1}$

12. Suppose the green triangle is $\frac{1}{2}$ of the whole. Which pattern block is

a. 1 whole?  **blue rhombus**     b. $1\frac{1}{2}$ wholes?  **red trapezoid**

13. Liam had 9 quarters. He spent $\frac{2}{3}$ of them on video games.

a. How many quarters did he spend?  **6** quarters

b. How much money does he have left?  **75 cents**

Use with Lesson 7.13.

402

Name                    Date          Time

## Unit 8 Checking Progress

1. If you wanted to build a fence around your backyard, would you find the
backyard's perimeter or its area? __perimeter__

2. What is the area of the polygon at
the right?

Area = __12__ square centimeters

1 cm

### Formulas

| Rectangle | Parallelogram | Triangle |
|---|---|---|
| Area = base * height | Area = base * height | Area = $\frac{1}{2}$ * (base * height) |

Complete the following. Measure each polygon with a centimeter ruler.

3. base = __4__ cm
   height = __3__ cm
   perimeter = __14__ cm
   Area = __12__ cm²

4. base = __3__ cm
   height = __2__ cm
   perimeter = __12__ cm
   Area = __6__ cm²

5. base = __3__ cm
   height = __2__ cm
   perimeter = __8__ cm
   Area = __3__ cm²

Use with Lesson 8.9.

404

---

Name                    Date          Time

## Unit 7 Checking Progress (cont.)    Sample answer:

14. Make a spinner.

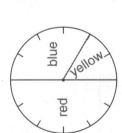
red
blue
yellow

a. Color it so that the paper clip will land on red
about $\frac{1}{2}$ of the time and on blue about $\frac{1}{3}$ of the
time. Color the remaining parts yellow. Try to
make an interesting design.

b. About what fraction of the
time do you think the paper
clip will land on yellow?

$\frac{1}{6}$

15. Use a paper clip and a pencil. Spin the paper clip
30 times on your new spinner.

a. Record the results in the table below.

| Color | Number of Times Clip Landed There | Fraction of Times Clip Landed There |
|---|---|---|
| red | | |
| blue | | |
| yellow | | |

b. Were the results what you expected? _____ Explain.
   Answers vary.

16. Queen Esther wants to divide her kingdom so that her oldest daughter
gets $\frac{1}{2}$ of it and her two youngest children each get $\frac{1}{3}$.

a. Can she do it? __no__

b. Explain your answer. Use your pattern blocks to help you answer the question.
   Sample answer: The sum of $\frac{1}{2}$ and $\frac{2}{3}$ is
   more than 1 or more than a whole.

c. Can you think of a better way to divide the kingdom? Explain.
   Answers vary.

Use with Lesson 7.13.

403

## Unit 9 Checking Progress

Name _____ Date _____ Time _____

1. Gloria made 15 out of 20 shots in the school basketball free-throw contest.

   a. What fraction of the shots did she make? $\dfrac{15}{20}$, or $\dfrac{3}{4}$

   b. What percent of the shots did she make? 75%

   c. At this rate, how many shots would she make if she took 100 shots? 75 shots

2. Jimmy set a goal of jogging a total of 100 miles over the summer. He filled in the square at the right to keep track of the miles he ran. During the first two weeks of June, he jogged 20 miles.

   a. What fraction of 100 miles did he jog in 2 weeks? $\dfrac{20}{100}$, $\dfrac{2}{10}$, or $\dfrac{1}{5}$

   b. What percent of 100 miles did he jog? 20%

   c. At this rate, how many weeks will it take him to jog 100 miles? 10 weeks

3. Fill in the table of equivalent fractions, decimals, and percents.

| Fraction | Decimal | Percent |
|---|---|---|
| $\dfrac{3}{10}$ | 0.30 | 30% |
| $\dfrac{1}{2}$ | 0.50 | 50% |
| $\dfrac{1}{4}$ | 0.25 | 25% |
| $\dfrac{3}{4}$ | 0.75 | 75% |
| $\dfrac{4}{5}$ | 0.80 | 80% |
| $\dfrac{5}{5}$ | 1.00 | 100% |

Use with Lesson 9.10.

406

---

## Unit 8 Checking Progress (cont.)

Name _____ Date _____ Time _____

6. Mrs. Lopez wants to tile her dining room floor. The room is 12 feet wide and 21 feet long. How many 1-square-foot tiles does she need to cover the floor?

   Answer: 252 tiles

7. Suppose Mrs. Lopez chooses tiles that are 6 inches on each side. How many 6-inch tiles would she need in order to cover her dining room floor?

   Answer: 1,008 tiles

   6 in.
   6 in.

   Explain how you got your answer.
   It takes four 6-inch tiles to cover one 12-inch tile, so she would need 4 * 252 tiles = 1,008 tiles.

Below is a scale drawing of a very large forest. A river runs along the northwest border of the forest. Use the scale to answer the following questions:

Scale: $\dfrac{1}{4}$ inch represents 10 miles

8. What is the length of the river along the northwest border?

   About 50 miles

9. What is the perimeter of the boundary of the forest?

   About 260 miles

10. How many square miles does each little square in the scale drawing represent?

   About 100 square miles

11. What is the area of the forest?

   About 4,300 square miles

Use with Lesson 8.9.

405

Name                    Date                    Time

## Unit 9 Checking Progress (cont.)

4. Use a calculator to rename each fraction as a decimal.

   a. $\frac{7}{16}$ = __0.4375__   b. $\frac{3}{25}$ = __0.12__   c. $\frac{6}{32}$ = __0.1875__

5. Use a calculator to rename each fraction as a percent.

   a. $\frac{3}{8}$ = __37.5__ %   b. $\frac{15}{16}$ = __93.75__ %   c. $\frac{3}{96}$ = __3.125__ %

6. Shade 40% of the square at the right.

   a. What fraction of the square did you shade?

   $\frac{40}{100}, \frac{4}{10}, \text{ or } \frac{2}{5}$

   b. Write this fraction as a decimal.   __0.40, or $\frac{4}{10}$__

   c. What percent of the square is *not* shaded?   __60%__

7. Susan bought a coat that sold for $150. She had a coupon for a 10% discount.

   a. How much money did she save with the discount?   __$15__

   b. How much did she pay for the coat?   __$135__

8. Randy is buying a color television. The television he wants costs $200 at both L-Mart and Al's Department Store. After Christmas, L-Mart put it on sale at a savings of $\frac{1}{4}$ off the regular price. Al's Department Store offered a 30% discount on all items.

   At which store should Randy buy the television?

   __Al's Department Store__

   Why?

   __Sample answer: Al's: A 30% discount on $200 is $60.__

   __L-Mart: $\frac{1}{4}$ = 25%. A 25% discount on $200 is $50.__

Use with Lesson 9.10.

407

---

Name                    Date                    Time

## Unit 9 Checking Progress (cont.)

Use an estimation strategy to multiply. Show your work.

9. 4.7 * 25 = __117.5__

10. 0.98 * 63 = __61.74__

11. __717.5__ = 205 * 3.5

Use an estimation strategy to divide. Show your work.

12. 48.6 / 6 = __8.1__

13. __40.3__ = 322.4 / 8

14. __0.75__ = 5.25 / 7

Use with Lesson 9.10.

408

Name                    Date                    Time

## Unit 10 Checking Progress

Use your Geometry Template to complete Problems 1–4.

**1.** Draw a shape that has no lines of symmetry.
Sample answers:

**2.** Draw a shape that has exactly 1 line of symmetry.
Sample answers:

**3.** Draw a shape that has exactly 2 lines of symmetry.
Sample answers:

**4.** Draw a shape that has more than 2 lines of symmetry.
Sample answers:

**5.** Which figure below is a reflection (flip) of the original figure? __B__

Original    A    B    C

**6.** Which figure below is a translation (slide) of the original figure? __C__

Original    A    B    C

Use with Lesson 10.7.

409

---

Name                    Date                    Time

## Unit 10 Checking Progress (cont.)

**7.** Which figure below shows the original figure rotated (turned) clockwise $\frac{1}{4}$ turn? __B__

Original    A    B    C

**8.** Use a transparent mirror to draw the reflection of the preimage.

preimage          image
line of reflection

**9.** Use a transparent mirror to draw the other half of the figure across the line of symmetry.

line of symmetry

**10.** Add.

a. $4 + 8 = $ __12__

b. $5 + (-2) = $ __3__

c. __−10__ $= -4 + (-6)$

d. __−6__ $= -9 + 3$

Use with Lesson 10.7.

410

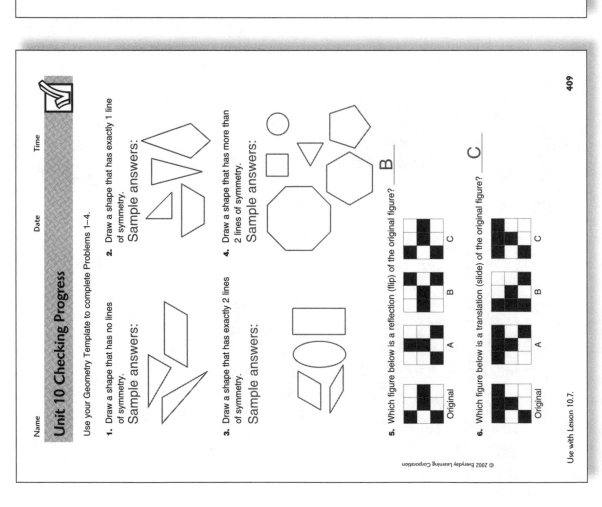

# Unit 11 Checking Progress

Name                    Date                    Time

1. Each object below has the shape of a geometric solid. Name the geometric solid.

   a.   sphere

   b.   cylinder

2. How many faces does the pentagonal pyramid have? 6 faces

3. Mark Xs on the vertices of the triangular prism.

4. How many edges does the rectangular pyramid have? 8 edges

5. Name the shape of the base of the pyramid below. hexagon

Use with Lesson 11.8.

---

# Unit 11 Checking Progress (cont.)

Name                    Date                    Time

6. Find the volume of each stack of centimeter cubes.

   a.   Volume = 48 cm³

   b.   Volume = 45 cm³

7. Calculate the volume of each rectangular prism.

   a. (3 cm, 9 cm, 7 cm)   Volume = 189 cm³

   b. (8 m, 5 m, 4 m)   Volume = 160 m³

8. Add.

   a. 14 + (-8) = 6

   b. (-20) + 9 = -11

   c. -18 = -5 + (-13)

   d. 0 = 6 + (-6)

9. Subtract.

   a. -10 - (-7) = -3

   b. -12 - (+7) = -19

   c. 2 = -6 - (-8)

   d. 17 = 14 - (-3)

10. Circle the most reasonable estimate for each weight.

    a. A box of cereal might weigh about    1.8 oz    (18 oz)    180 oz

    b. A pencil might weigh about    0.7 g    (7 g)    70 g

    c. A female adult might weigh about    (65 kg)    650 kg    6,500 kg

Use with Lesson 11.8.

Name                                    Date                Time

## Unit 12 Checking Progress

1. It was reported that on New Year's Day, 1907, Theodore Roosevelt shook hands with 8,513 people. Does this seem reasonable? Explain your answer.
**Sample answer: This seems reasonable. At a rate of 10 handshakes per minute, that would yield 10 * 60 * 14 = 8,400 handshakes in a 14-hour period.**

2. Tina works 7 hours a day, 5 days a week. She earns $56.00 per day.

   a. How much does she earn per hour? **$8.00**

   b. How much does she earn per week? **$280.00**

3. The Davis family drove 280 miles to visit relatives. It took 5 hours. At that rate, how many miles had the Davises driven in 3 hours? **168** miles

   Fill in the rate table, if needed.

| Hours | 1 | 2 | 3 | 4 | 5 |
|-------|----|-----|-----|-----|-----|
| Miles | 56 | 112 | 168 | 224 | 280 |

4. A store charges $1.49 for a 20-ounce box of Puff Flakes cereal and $1.72 for a 24-ounce box of the same cereal. Which is the better buy? **The 24-ounce box**

   Explain why.
   **Sample answer: The 20-ounce box costs 7.5¢ per ounce, and the 24-ounce box costs only 7.2¢ per ounce.**

Use with Lesson 12.7.                    413

---

Name                                    Date                Time

## Unit 12 Checking Progress (cont.)

5. Use the sign at the right to help you make good decisions. Solve the problems. Explain how you found your answers.

45 cents each
6 for $2.50
$4.80 a dozen

DOUGHNUTS

   a. Joey goes to Doreen's Delicious Doughnuts to buy doughnuts for the class party. What is the least amount of money he will have to pay for 30 doughnuts?
   **$12.10**

   Explain.
   **Sample answer: If Joey buys two dozen at $4.80 per dozen and 6 for $2.50, the total cost will be (2 * $4.80) + $2.50 = $12.10.**

   b. Pretend that your mother sent you to buy 11 doughnuts. If you had enough money, would you buy a dozen doughnuts instead? Explain.
   **Sample answer: Yes. 11 doughnuts would cost $2.50 + (5 * $0.45) = $4.75. For 5 cents more, I could buy a dozen doughnuts. Buying one extra doughnut for only 5 cents is a good deal.**

6. Make up a rate number story. Then solve it.
   **Sample answer: Jeanine can ride her bike 8 miles per hour. At that rate, how long would it take her to ride to her grandmother's house, 6 miles away?**

   Answer: ____**45 min**____
                  (unit)

414                                      Use with Lesson 12.7.

Name _____ Date _____ Time _____

## Midyear Assessment

Add, subtract, or multiply.

1. Lisa's team had a cookie sale. During the first week of the sale, the girls sold 560 boxes of cookies. During the last week, they sold 138 boxes. How many boxes did they sell in all?

**698 boxes**

2. A gallon of 2% milk costs $2.19 at the Gem supermarket and $2.45 at the 6-to-Midnight convenience store. How much more does a gallon of milk cost at the convenience store?

**$0.26**

Solve each problem. Show your work.

3. $653 - 289 =$ **364**

4. **830** $= 551 + 279$

5. **896** $= 7 * 128$

6. $49 * 67 =$ **3,283**

7. Make up a number story using the information below. Then solve the problem and write a number model.

- At Bloom's Flower Shop, roses cost 99 cents each.
- A dozen roses costs $10.00.
- Carnations cost 49 cents each or 3 for a dollar.

Sample problem: Zach has $9.50. Can he buy 9 carnations and 6 roses?

Answer: Sample answer: Yes, but he will only have 56¢ left for tax. To be safe, he should probably buy 5 roses.

Number model:
$(3 * \$1) + (6 * \$0.99) = \$8.94$

Use with Lesson 6.11.

---

Name _____ Date _____ Time _____

## Midyear Assessment (cont.)

8. Write each number with digits.

a. Twelve thousand, five hundred sixty-five **12,565**

b. Four million, six hundred thousand, twenty-seven **4,600,027**

c. Twelve and four tenths **12.4**

d. Five and sixteen hundredths **5.16**

9. Each of the following names describes one of the geometric figures below.

parallel lines        concentric circles        rectangle
regular polygon        right angle        trapezoid

Write the correct name below the picture.

a.

**right angle**

b.

**trapezoid**

c.

**parallel lines**

d.

**concentric circles**

e.

**regular polygon**

f.

**rectangle**

10. Draw $\overleftrightarrow{QR}$ parallel to $\overleftrightarrow{ST}$. Draw line segment $WX$ so that it intersects ray $QR$ and line $ST$.

Use with Lesson 6.11.

## Page 417

Name _____ Date _____ Time _____

### Midyear Assessment (cont.)

**11.** As part of her science project on sleep, Jeannie asked 13 students in her class how many hours they had slept the night before, to the nearest half-hour. Here are the results of her survey.

Number of hours of sleep: 7, 7.5, 8, 8, 8, 8.5, 9, 9, 9.5, 10, 10, 10.5

**a.** What is the median number of hours the students slept? __8.5__

**b.** What is the mode? __8__

**c.** What is the minimum number of hours slept? __7__

**d.** What is the maximum number of hours slept? __10.5__

**e.** What is the range of hours they slept? __3.5__

**12.** Circle the best estimate for each of the following measurements.

**a.** The width of my palm       8 mm       (8 cm)       8 m

**b.** The height of a doorway       (2 m)       20 m       200 m

**c.** The thickness of a penny       1 m       1 cm       (1 mm)

**d.** The length of a book       1 in.       (1 ft)       1 yd

**13.** Use your protractor. Measure each angle below to the nearest degree.

**a.**

∠ABC measures __40__ °.

It is an ( (acute) or obtuse ) angle.

**b.**

∠DEF measures __120__ °.

It is an ( acute or (obtuse) ) angle.

## Page 418

Name _____ Date _____ Time _____

### Midyear Assessment (cont.)

**14.** Measure the line segment to the nearest centimeter and to the nearest millimeter.

**a.** __7__ cm

**b.** __68__ mm

**15.** Measure the line segment to the nearest inch.

__5__ in.

**16.** Measure the line segment to the nearest $\frac{1}{2}$ inch.

$3\frac{1}{2}$ in.

**17.** Find the solution of each open sentence.

**a.** $53 = x + 25$

Solution: $x = 28$

**b.** $7 * y = 42$       Solution: $y = 6$

**c.** $m / 9 = 5$       Solution: $m = 45$

**18.** Divide. If there is a remainder, report it as a fraction. Show your work.

**a.** $385 \div 7 =$ __55__

**b.** $6\overline{)572} =$ $95\frac{1}{3}$

**19.** Tell whether each number sentence is true or false.

**a.** $(5 * 6) + 13 = 43$ __true__

**b.** $(81 / 9) - (36 / 4) = 3$ __false__

**c.** $(12 - 6) * 3^2 = 36$ __false__

**d.** $30 - (4 * 7) = 2$ __true__

## End-of-Year Assessment

Solve the problems. Don't forget to write the unit in your answer when it is needed.

1. Study the figure at the right. For each statement below, write true or false.

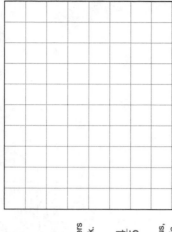

   a. This figure is a rectangle. __false__
   b. This figure is a polygon. __true__
   c. The opposite sides are parallel. __true__
   d. All angles are right angles. __false__

2. Joe and Shawna are setting up chairs for an assembly. They make 9 rows with 7 chairs in each row. How many chairs have they set up? __63 chairs__

3. The Smiths are driving at about 50 miles per hour. At that rate,
   a. how far will they drive in half an hour? __25 miles__
   b. how far will they drive in 4 hours? __200 miles__

4. Find the solution of each open sentence.
   a. $8 * x = 32$
      Solution: __$x = 4$__
   b. $y - 27 = 55$
      Solution: __$y = 82$__
   c. $108 + r = 150$
      Solution: __$r = 42$__

5. Corrine left home at 10:40 A.M. to go to soccer practice. She got back from practice at 12:15 P.M. How long had she been gone? __95 minutes__

Use with Lesson 12.7.

419

---

## End-of-Year Assessment (cont.)

6. Multiply. Show your work.
   a. $147 * 5 =$ __735__
   b. $126 * 40 =$ __5,040__

7. Divide. Report any remainders as fractions. Show your work.
   a. $438 / 6 =$ __73__
   b. $5\overline{)329} =$ __$65\frac{8}{10}$, or $65\frac{4}{5}$__

8. According to the 1990 census, the population of Philadelphia was one million, five hundred eighty-five thousand, five hundred seventy-seven.
   a. Write this number with digits. __1,585,577__
   b. Is the number more or less than $10^4$? __More than__
   c. Round the number to the nearest thousand. __1,586,000__

9. Use your centimeter ruler to measure the sides of the rectangle at the right to the nearest $\frac{1}{2}$ cm.
   a. Length = about __8 cm__
   b. Width = about __4.5 cm__
   c. Perimeter = about __25 cm__
   d. Area = about __36 cm²__

length
width

Use with Lesson 12.7.

420

Name _____ Date _____ Time _____

## End-of-Year Assessment (cont.)

10. Bob kept a record for a week of how many hours the TV was on in his house. He showed this information in the following bar graph.

**Number of Hours the TV Was on in My House for 1 Week**

a. On Wednesday, how many hours was the TV on? __2.5 hours__

b. On what day was the TV on for the *maximum* number of hours? __Sat.__

c. On what day was the TV on for the *minimum* number of hours? __Fri.__

d. On what day was the TV on for the *median* number of hours? __Mon.__

11. a. Color $\frac{1}{4}$ of the spinner at the right.

b. What fraction of the spinner is *not* colored? __$\frac{3}{4}$__

c. What *percent* of the spinner is colored? __25%__

d. If you spin the spinner 100 times, about how many times would you expect it to land on the colored part? __25 times__

e. If you spin the spinner 300 times, about how many times would you expect it to land on the colored part? __75 times__

---

Name _____ Date _____ Time _____

## End-of-Year Assessment (cont.)

12. a. Circle $\frac{3}{4}$ of the stars.

b. Write two fractions that are equivalent to $\frac{3}{4}$. __Sample answers:__ $\frac{9}{12}, \frac{6}{8}$

c. Write the decimal that is equivalent to $\frac{3}{4}$. __0.75__

d. Write the percent that is equivalent to $\frac{3}{4}$. __75%__

13. Write <, >, or =.

a. $\frac{3}{5}$ > $\frac{2}{5}$

b. $\frac{1}{4}$ > $\frac{1}{6}$

c. $\frac{9}{10}$ > $\frac{2}{3}$

d. $\frac{3}{10}$ > 0.03

e. $\frac{6}{10}$ = 0.6

f. $\frac{37}{100}$ > 0.2

g. 1.2 > 1.096

h. $10^3$ < 3 million

14. Circle the shapes that have exactly 1 line of symmetry.

## End-of-Year Assessment (cont.)

**15.** The objects below have the shapes of geometric solids. Name the solids.

a.  TENNIS BALLS

cylinder

b.  FACIAL TISSUES

rectangular prism

**16.** Add or subtract.

a. $\frac{4}{5}$ = $\frac{1}{5} + \frac{3}{5}$

b. $\frac{6}{4}$, or $1\frac{1}{2}$ = $\frac{3}{4} + \frac{3}{4}$

c. $\frac{3}{4} - \frac{1}{4}$ = $\frac{2}{4}$, or $\frac{1}{2}$

d. $\frac{9}{10} - \frac{3}{10}$ = $\frac{6}{10}$, or $\frac{3}{5}$

**17.** Estimate. Is the sum or difference closest to 0, 1, or 2?

a. $\frac{1}{5} + \frac{1}{8}$    0

b. $1\frac{2}{13} + \frac{1}{2}$    2

c. $2\frac{1}{12} - \frac{9}{10}$    1

d. $\frac{7}{8} - \frac{5}{6}$    0

Use with Lesson 12.7.

---

## End-of-Year Assessment (cont.)

**18.** Add or subtract.

a. $-5 + (-9) =$ $-14$

b. $-12 + 7 =$ $-5$

c. $10 + (-4) =$ $6$

d. $-8 + 8 =$ $0$

e. $-8 - (+7) =$ $-15$

f. $9 - (-3) =$ $12$

g. $-10 - (-2) =$ $-8$

h. $-7 - (-9) =$ $2$

Use these formulas to calculate the areas of the figures below.

| Parallelogram: | Triangle: |
|---|---|
| Area = base * height | Area = $\frac{1}{2}$ of (base * height) |

**19.**  7 cm, 9 cm

Area = $63$ cm²

**20.**  4 in., 6 in.

Area = $12$ in.²

**21.** What is the volume of the storage bin shown at the right?

 STORAGE BIN  3 feet, 2 feet, 3.5 feet

Volume = $21$ ft³

**22.** Which figure shows the original figure rotated counterclockwise $\frac{1}{4}$ turn?

B

 Original        A        B        C

Use with Lesson 12.7.

Assessment Masters

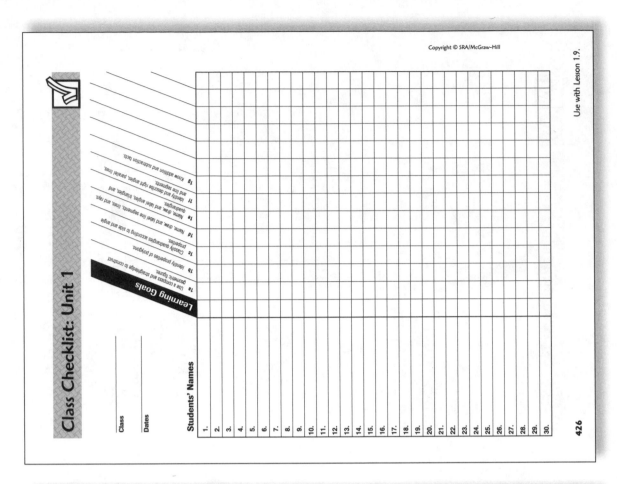

## Class Checklist: Unit 1

Class _____

Dates _____

**Learning Goals**

1a Use a compass and straightedge to construct geometric figures.

1b Identify properties of polygons.

1c Classify quadrangles according to side and angle properties.

1d Name, draw, and label line segments, lines, and rays.

1e Name, draw, and label line segments, lines, and rays. quadrangles.

1f Identify and describe right angles, triangles, and quadrangles.

1g Identify and describe right angles, parallel lines, and line segments.

1h Know addition and subtraction facts.

**Students' Names**

1.
2.
3.
4.
5.
6.
7.
8.
9.
10.
11.
12.
13.
14.
15.
16.
17.
18.
19.
20.
21.
22.
23.
24.
25.
26.
27.
28.
29.
30.

Use with Lesson 1.9.

426

---

Name _____ Date _____ Time _____

## End-of-Year Assessment (cont.)

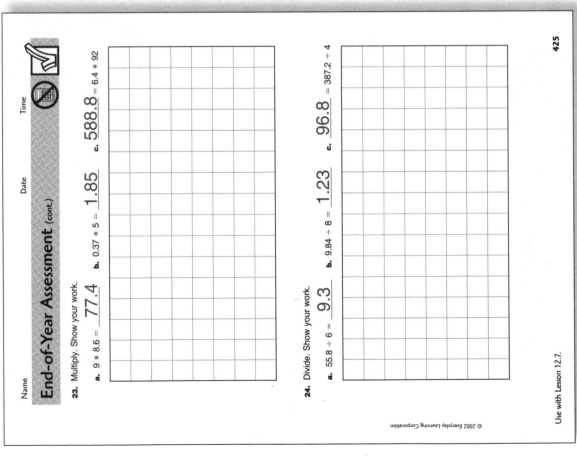

**23.** Multiply. Show your work.

a. $9 * 8.6 = \underline{77.4}$

b. $0.37 * 5 = \underline{1.85}$

c. $\underline{588.8} = 6.4 * 92$

**24.** Divide. Show your work.

a. $55.8 \div 6 = \underline{9.3}$

b. $9.84 \div 8 = \underline{1.23}$

c. $\underline{96.8} = 387.2 \div 4$

Use with Lesson 12.7.

425

Assessment Masters

## Class Checklist: Unit 2

Class _____

Dates _____

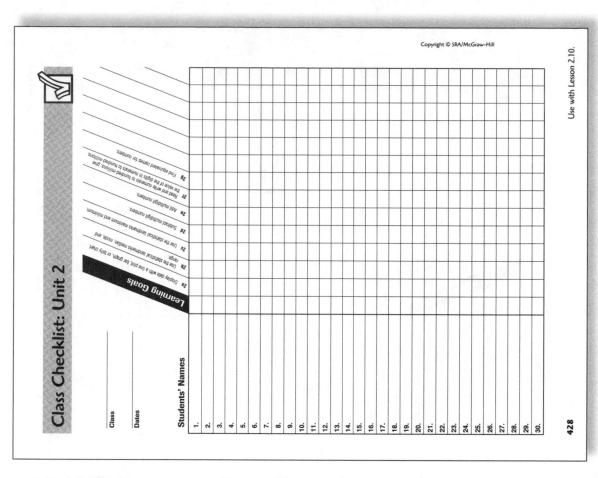

| Learning Goals | | | | | | | |
|---|---|---|---|---|---|---|---|
| 2a Display data with a line plot, bar graph, or tally chart. | 2b Use the statistical landmarks median, mode, and range. | 2c Use the statistical landmarks maximum and minimum. | 2d Subtract multidigit numbers. | 2e Add multidigit numbers. | 2f Read and write numerals to hundred-millions; give the value of the digits in numerals to hundred-millions. | 2g Find equivalent names for numbers. | |

**Students' Names**

1.
2.
3.
4.
5.
6.
7.
8.
9.
10.
11.
12.
13.
14.
15.
16.
17.
18.
19.
20.
21.
22.
23.
24.
25.
26.
27.
28.
29.
30.

Use with Lesson 2.10.

428

---

Student's Name _____  Date _____

## Individual Profile of Progress: Unit 1

| Check ✔ | | | Learning Goals | Comments |
|---|---|---|---|---|
| B | D | S | | |
| | | | 1a Use a compass and straightedge to construct geometric figures. | |
| | | | 1b Identify properties of polygons. | |
| | | | 1c Classify quadrangles according to side and angle properties. | |
| | | | 1d Name, draw, and label line segments, lines, and rays. | |
| | | | 1e Name, draw, and label angles, triangles, and quadrangles. | |
| | | | 1f Identify and describe right angles, parallel lines, and line segments. | |
| | | | 1g Know addition and subtraction facts. | |

**Notes to Parents**

B = Beginning; D = Developing; S = Secure

Use with Lesson 1.9.

427

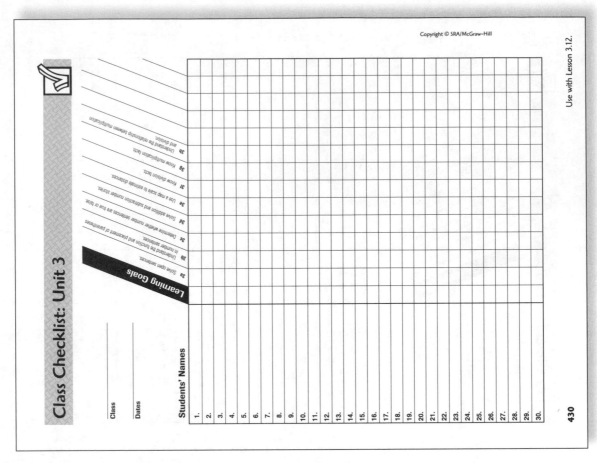

## Class Checklist: Unit 3

Class _____

Dates _____

**Learning Goals**

3a Solve open sentences.
3b Understand the function and placement of parentheses in number sentences.
3c Determine whether number sentences are true or false.
3d Solve addition and subtraction number stories.
3e Use a map scale to estimate distances.
3f Know division facts.
3g Know multiplication facts.
3h Understand the relationship between multiplication and division.

**Students' Names**

1.
2.
3.
4.
5.
6.
7.
8.
9.
10.
11.
12.
13.
14.
15.
16.
17.
18.
19.
20.
21.
22.
23.
24.
25.
26.
27.
28.
29.
30.

Use with Lesson 3.12.

430

---

Student's Name _____ Date _____

## Individual Profile of Progress: Unit 2

**Check ✓**

| B | D | S | Learning Goals | Comments |
|---|---|---|---|---|
| | | | 2a Display data with a line plot, bar graph, or tally chart. | |
| | | | 2b Use the statistical landmarks median, mode, and range. | |
| | | | 2c Use the statistical landmarks maximum and minimum. | |
| | | | 2d Subtract multidigit numbers. | |
| | | | 2e Add multidigit numbers. | |
| | | | 2f Read and write numerals to hundred-millions; give the value of the digits in numerals to hundred-millions. | |
| | | | 2g Find equivalent names for numbers. | |

**Notes to Parents**

B = **Beginning**; D = **Developing**; S = **Secure**

Use with Lesson 2.10.

429

# Class Checklist: Unit 4

Class _____

Dates _____

**Learning Goals**

4a Express metric measures with decimals.

4b Convert between metric measures.

4c Read and write decimals to thousandths.

4d Compare and order decimals.

4e Draw and measure line segments to the nearest millimeter.

4f Use personal references to estimate lengths in metric units.

4g Solve 1- and 2-place decimal addition and subtraction problems and number stories.

4h Draw and measure line segments to the nearest centimeter.

4i Use dollars-and-cents notation.

**Students' Names**

1.
2.
3.
4.
5.
6.
7.
8.
9.
10.
11.
12.
13.
14.
15.
16.
17.
18.
19.
20.
21.
22.
23.
24.
25.
26.
27.
28.
29.
30.

Use with Lesson 4.11.

432

---

Student's Name _____

Date _____

# Individual Profile of Progress: Unit 3

**Check ✓** B D S

| | Learning Goals | Comments |
|---|---|---|
| 3a | Solve open sentences. | |
| 3b | Understand the function and placement of parentheses in number sentences. | |
| 3c | Determine whether number sentences are true or false. | |
| 3d | Solve addition and subtraction number stories. | |
| 3e | Use a map scale to estimate distances. | |
| 3f | Know division facts. | |
| 3g | Know multiplication facts. | |
| 3h | Understand the relationship between multiplication and division. | |

**Notes to Parents**

_____

_____

_____

_____

B = Beginning; D = Developing; S = Secure

Use with Lesson 3.12.

431

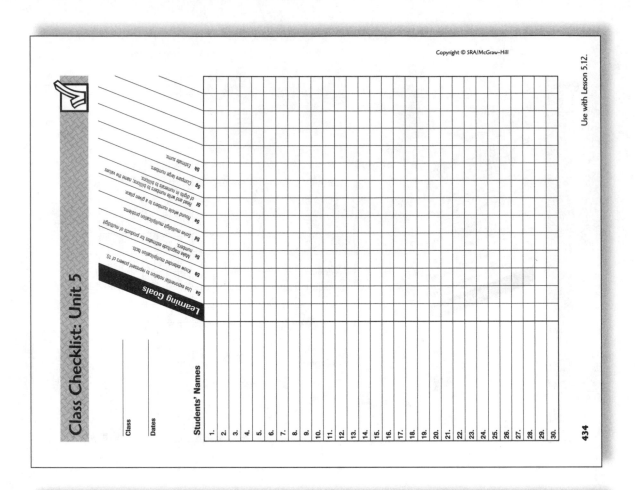

## Class Checklist: Unit 5

Class _____

Dates _____

### Learning Goals

- **5a** Use exponential notation to represent powers of 10.
- **5b** Know extended multiplication facts.
- **5c** Make magnitude estimates for products of multidigit numbers.
- **5d** Solve multidigit multiplication problems.
- **5e** Round whole numbers to a given place.
- **5f** Read and write numbers to billions; name the values of digits in numerals to billions.
- **5g** Compare large numbers.
- **5h** Estimate sums.

**Students' Names**

1.
2.
3.
4.
5.
6.
7.
8.
9.
10.
11.
12.
13.
14.
15.
16.
17.
18.
19.
20.
21.
22.
23.
24.
25.
26.
27.
28.
29.
30.

Use with Lesson 5.12.

434

---

Student's Name _____  Date _____

## Individual Profile of Progress: Unit 4

| Check ✓ | | | Learning Goals | Comments |
|---|---|---|---|---|
| **B** | **D** | **S** | | |
| | | | **4a** Express metric measures with decimals. | |
| | | | **4b** Convert between metric measures. | |
| | | | **4c** Read and write decimals to thousandths. | |
| | | | **4d** Compare and order decimals. | |
| | | | **4e** Draw and measure line segments to the nearest millimeter. | |
| | | | **4f** Use personal references to estimate lengths in metric units. | |
| | | | **4g** Solve 1- and 2-place decimal addition and subtraction problems and number stories. | |
| | | | **4h** Draw and measure line segments to the nearest centimeter. | |
| | | | **4i** Use dollars-and-cents notation. | |

**Notes to Parents**

**B** = Beginning; **D** = Developing; **S** = Secure

Use with Lesson 4.11.

433

## Class Checklist: Unit 6

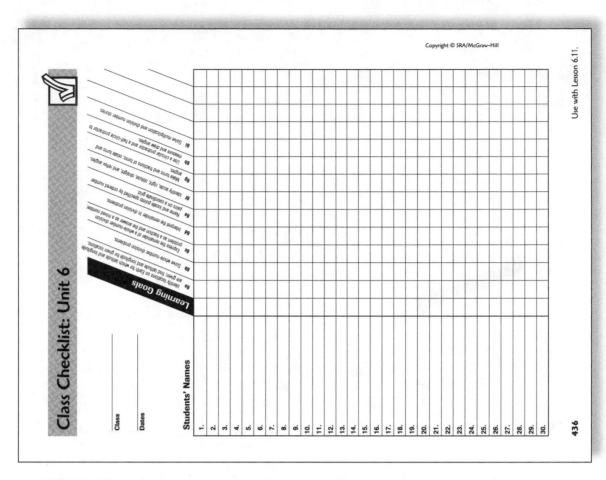

Class _____

Dates _____

**Learning Goals**

6a Identify locations on Earth for which latitude and longitude are given; find latitude and longitude for given location.

6b Solve whole-number division problems.

6c Express the remainder in division problems.

6d Interpret the remainder of a whole-number division problem as a fraction and the answer as a mixed number.

6e Name and locate points specified by ordered number pairs on a coordinate grid.

6f Identify acute, right, obtuse, straight, and reflex angles.

6g Make turns and fractions of turns.

6h Use a circular protractor and a half-circle protractor to measure and draw angles.

6i Solve multiplication and division number stories.

**Students' Names**

1.
2.
3.
4.
5.
6.
7.
8.
9.
10.
11.
12.
13.
14.
15.
16.
17.
18.
19.
20.
21.
22.
23.
24.
25.
26.
27.
28.
29.
30.

436

Use with Lesson 6.11.

---

Student's Name _____   Date _____

## Individual Profile of Progress: Unit 5

| Check ✓ | | | Learning Goals | Comments |
|---|---|---|---|---|
| **B** | **D** | **S** | | |
| | | | 5a Use exponential notation to represent powers of 10. | |
| | | | 5b Know extended multiplication facts. | |
| | | | 5c Make magnitude estimates for products of multidigit numbers. | |
| | | | 5d Solve multidigit multiplication problems. | |
| | | | 5e Round whole numbers to a given place. | |
| | | | 5f Read and write numbers to billions; name the values of digits in numerals to billions. | |
| | | | 5g Compare large numbers. | |
| | | | 5h Estimate sums. | |

**Notes to Parents**

_____

_____

_____

_____

**B** = Beginning; **D** = Developing; **S** = Secure

Use with Lesson 5.12.

435

## Class Checklist: Unit 7

Class _____

Dates _____

**Learning Goals**

| Code | Goal |
|---|---|
| 7a | Add and subtract fractions. |
| 7b | Rename fractions with denominators of 10 and 100 as decimals. |
| 7c | Apply basic vocabulary and concepts associated with chance events. |
| 7d | Compare and order fractions. |
| 7e | Find equivalent fractions for given fractions. |
| 7f | Identify the whole for fractions. |
| 7g | Identify fractional parts of a collection of objects. |
| 7h | Identify fractional parts of regions. |

**Students' Names**

1.
2.
3.
4.
5.
6.
7.
8.
9.
10.
11.
12.
13.
14.
15.
16.
17.
18.
19.
20.
21.
22.
23.
24.
25.
26.
27.
28.
29.
30.

438

Use with Lesson 7.13.

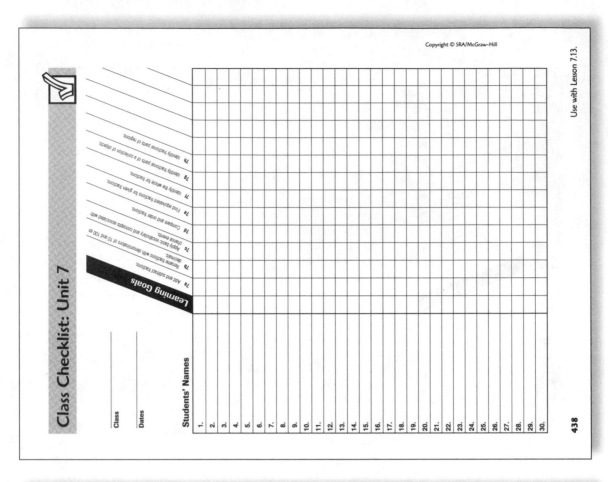

---

Student's Name _____  Date _____

## Individual Profile of Progress: Unit 6

| Check ✔ | | | Learning Goals | Comments |
|---|---|---|---|---|
| B | D | S | | |
| | | | 6a Identify locations on Earth for which latitude and longitude are given; find latitude and longitude for given locations. | |
| | | | 6b Solve whole-number division problems. | |
| | | | 6c Express the remainder of a whole-number division problem as a fraction and the answer as a mixed number. | |
| | | | 6d Interpret the remainder in division problems. | |
| | | | 6e Name and locate points specified by ordered number pairs on a coordinate grid. | |
| | | | 6f Identify acute, right, obtuse, straight, and reflex angles. | |
| | | | 6g Make turns and fractions of turns; relate turns and angles. | |
| | | | 6h Use a circular protractor and a half-circle protractor to measure and draw angles. | |
| | | | 6i Solve multiplication and division number stories. | |

**Notes to Parents**

_____

_____

_____

B = Beginning; D = Developing; S = Secure

Use with Lesson 6.11.

437

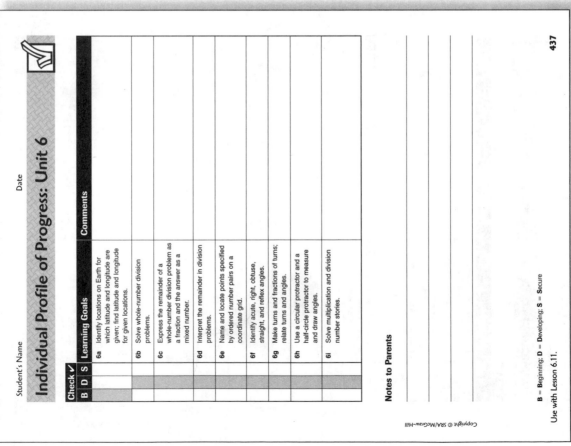

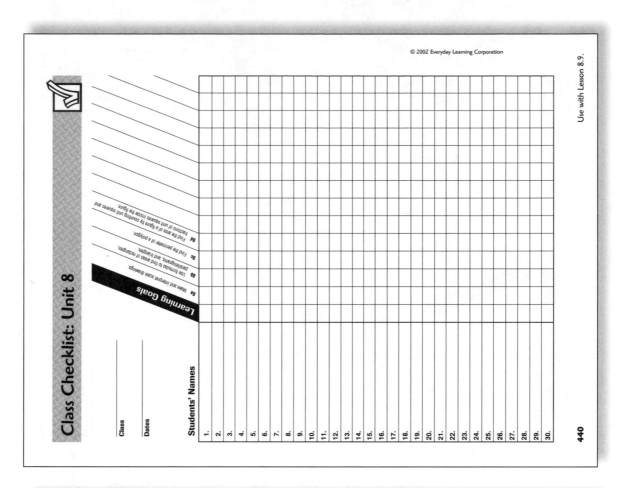

## Class Checklist: Unit 8

Class _____

Dates _____

**Learning Goals**

8a Make and interpret scale drawings.

8b Use formulas to find areas of rectangles, parallelograms, and triangles.

8c Find the perimeter of a polygon.

8d Find the area of a figure by counting unit squares and fractions of unit squares inside the figure.

**Students' Names**

1.
2.
3.
4.
5.
6.
7.
8.
9.
10.
11.
12.
13.
14.
15.
16.
17.
18.
19.
20.
21.
22.
23.
24.
25.
26.
27.
28.
29.
30.

© 2002 Everyday Learning Corporation

Use with Lesson 8.9.

440

---

Student's Name _____    Date _____

## Individual Profile of Progress: Unit 7

| Check ✔ | | | Learning Goals | Comments |
|---|---|---|---|---|
| B | D | S | | |
| | | | 7a Add and subtract fractions. | |
| | | | 7b Rename fractions with denominators of 10 and 100 as decimals. | |
| | | | 7c Apply basic vocabulary and concepts associated with chance events. | |
| | | | 7d Compare and order fractions. | |
| | | | 7e Find equivalent fractions for given fractions. | |
| | | | 7f Identify the whole for fractions. | |
| | | | 7g Identify fractional parts of a collection of objects. | |
| | | | 7h Identify fractional parts of regions. | |

**Notes to Parents**

_____
_____
_____
_____

B = Beginning; D = Developing; S = Secure

Use with Lesson 7.13.

Copyright © SRA/McGraw-Hill

439

Assessment Masters **103**

Assessment Masters

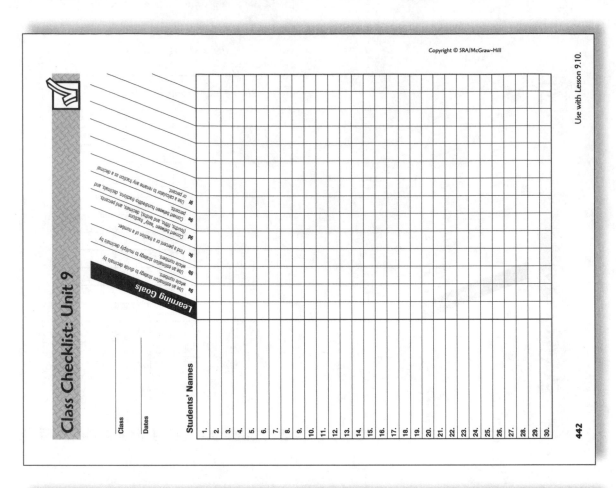

## Class Checklist: Unit 9

Class _____

Dates _____

**Learning Goals**

- **9a** Use an estimation strategy to divide decimals by whole numbers.
- **9b** Use an estimation strategy to multiply decimals by whole numbers.
- **9c** Find a percent or a fraction of a number.
- **9d** Convert between "easy" fractions (fourths, fifths, and tenths), decimals, and percents.
- **9e** Convert between hundredths-fraction, decimals, and percents.
- **9f** Use a calculator to rename any fraction as a decimal or percent.

**Students' Names**

1.
2.
3.
4.
5.
6.
7.
8.
9.
10.
11.
12.
13.
14.
15.
16.
17.
18.
19.
20.
21.
22.
23.
24.
25.
26.
27.
28.
29.
30.

442

Use with Lesson 9.10.

---

Student's Name _____    Date _____

## Individual Profile of Progress: Unit 8

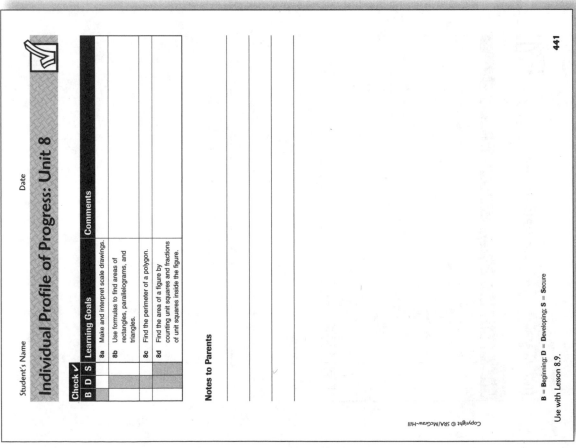

| Check ✔ | | | Learning Goals | Comments |
|---|---|---|---|---|
| B | D | S | | |
| | | | **8a** Make and interpret scale drawings. | |
| | | | **8b** Use formulas to find areas of rectangles, parallelograms, and triangles. | |
| | | | **8c** Find the perimeter of a polygon. | |
| | | | **8d** Find the area of a figure by counting unit squares and fractions of unit squares inside the figure. | |

**Notes to Parents**

B = Beginning; D = Developing; S = Secure

Use with Lesson 8.9.

441

## Class Checklist: Unit 10

Class

Dates

**Learning Goals**

10a Add integers.
10b Rotate figures.
10c Translate figures.
10d Use a transparent mirror to draw the reflection of a figure.
10e Identify lines of symmetry, lines of reflection, reflected figures, and figures with line symmetry.

**Students' Names**

1.
2.
3.
4.
5.
6.
7.
8.
9.
10.
11.
12.
13.
14.
15.
16.
17.
18.
19.
20.
21.
22.
23.
24.
25.
26.
27.
28.
29.
30.

Use with Lesson 10.7.

444

---

Student's Name

Date

## Individual Profile of Progress: Unit 9

| Check ✓ | | | Learning Goals | Comments |
|---|---|---|---|---|
| B | D | S | | |
| | | | 9a Use an estimation strategy to divide decimals by whole numbers. | |
| | | | 9b Use an estimation strategy to multiply decimals by whole numbers. | |
| | | | 9c Find a percent or a fraction of a number. | |
| | | | 9d Convert between "easy" fractions (fourths, fifths, and tenths), decimals, and percents. | |
| | | | 9e Convert between hundredths-fractions, decimals, and percents. | |
| | | | 9f Use a calculator to rename any fraction as a decimal or percent. | |

**Notes to Parents**

B = Beginning; D = Developing; S = Secure

Use with Lesson 9.10.

443

# Class Checklist: Unit 11

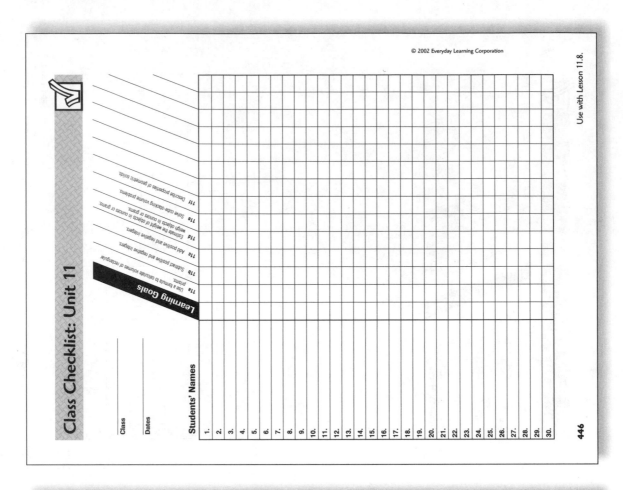

Class _____

Dates _____

## Learning Goals

| | 11a | Use a formula to calculate volumes of rectangular prisms. |
| | 11b | Subtract positive and negative integers. |
| | 11c | Add positive and negative integers. |
| | 11d | Estimate the weight of objects in ounces or grams; weigh objects in ounces or grams. |
| | 11e | Solve cube-stacking volume problems. |
| | 11f | Describe properties of geometric solids. |

### Students' Names

1.
2.
3.
4.
5.
6.
7.
8.
9.
10.
11.
12.
13.
14.
15.
16.
17.
18.
19.
20.
21.
22.
23.
24.
25.
26.
27.
28.
29.
30.

Use with Lesson 11.8.

446

---

Student's Name _____          Date _____

# Individual Profile of Progress: Unit 10

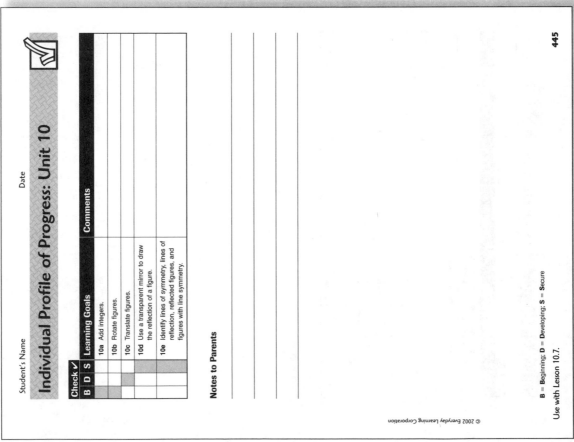

| Check ✔ | | | Learning Goals | Comments |
|---|---|---|---|---|
| B | D | S | | |
| | | | 10a  Add integers. | |
| | | | 10b  Rotate figures. | |
| | | | 10c  Translate figures. | |
| | | | 10d  Use a transparent mirror to draw the reflection of a figure. | |
| | | | 10e  Identify lines of symmetry, lines of reflection, reflected figures, and figures with line symmetry. | |

**Notes to Parents**

_____

_____

_____

B = Beginning; D = Developing; S = Secure

Use with Lesson 10.7.

445

## Class Checklist: Unit 12

Class

Dates

### Learning Goals

12a  Find unit rate.

12b  Calculate unit prices to determine which product is the "better buy."

12c  Evaluate reasonableness of rate data.

12d  Collect and compare rate data.

12e  Use rate tables, if necessary, to solve rate problems.

**Students' Names**

1.
2.
3.
4.
5.
6.
7.
8.
9.
10.
11.
12.
13.
14.
15.
16.
17.
18.
19.
20.
21.
22.
23.
24.
25.
26.
27.
28.
29.
30.

Use with Lesson 12.7.

448

---

Student's Name

Date

## Individual Profile of Progress: Unit 11

| Check ✓ | | | Learning Goals | Comments |
|---|---|---|---|---|
| B | D | S | | |
| | | | 11a  Use a formula to calculate volumes of rectangular prisms. | |
| | | | 11b  Subtract positive and negative integers. | |
| | | | 11c  Add positive and negative integers. | |
| | | | 11d  Estimate the weight of objects in ounces or grams; weigh objects in ounces or grams. | |
| | | | 11e  Solve cube-stacking volume problems. | |
| | | | 11f  Describe properties of geometric solids. | |

**Notes to Parents**

B = Beginning; **D** = Developing; **S** = Secure

Use with Lesson 11.8.

447

## Class Checklist: 1st Quarter

Class _____

Dates _____

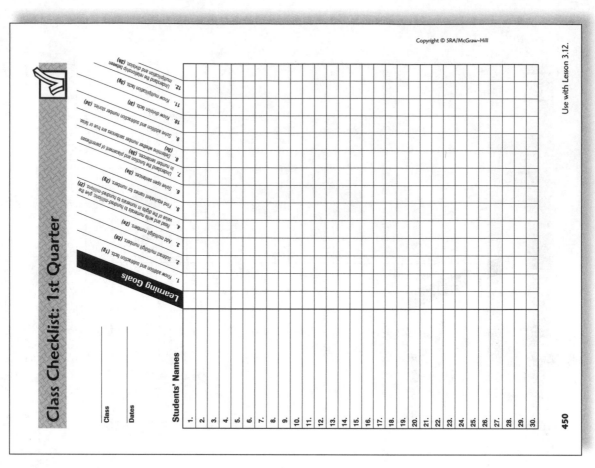

### Learning Goals

1. Know addition and subtraction facts. (1a)
2. Subtract multidigit numbers. (2d)
3. Add multidigit numbers. (2c)
4. Read and write numerals to hundred-millions; give the value of the digits in numerals to hundred-millions. (2z)
5. Find equivalent names for numbers. (2y)
6. Solve open sentences. (2e)
7. Understand the function and placement of parentheses in number sentences. (3b)
8. Determine whether number sentences are true or false. (3c)
9. Solve addition and subtraction number stories. (3d)
10. Know division facts. (3i)
11. Know multiplication facts. (3g)
12. Understand the relationship between multiplication and division. (3h)

### Students' Names

1. 2. 3. 4. 5. 6. 7. 8. 9. 10. 11. 12. 13. 14. 15. 16. 17. 18. 19. 20. 21. 22. 23. 24. 25. 26. 27. 28. 29. 30.

Use with Lesson 3.12.

450

---

Student's Name _____ Date _____

## Individual Profile of Progress: Unit 12

| Check ✔ | | | Learning Goals | Comments |
|---|---|---|---|---|
| B | D | S | | |
| | | | 12a Find unit rates. | |
| | | | 12b Calculate unit prices to determine which product is the "better buy." | |
| | | | 12c Evaluate reasonableness of rate data. | |
| | | | 12d Collect and compare rate data. | |
| | | | 12e Use rate tables, if necessary, to solve rate problems. | |

**Notes to Parents**

B = Beginning; D = Developing; S = Secure

Use with Lesson 12.7.

449

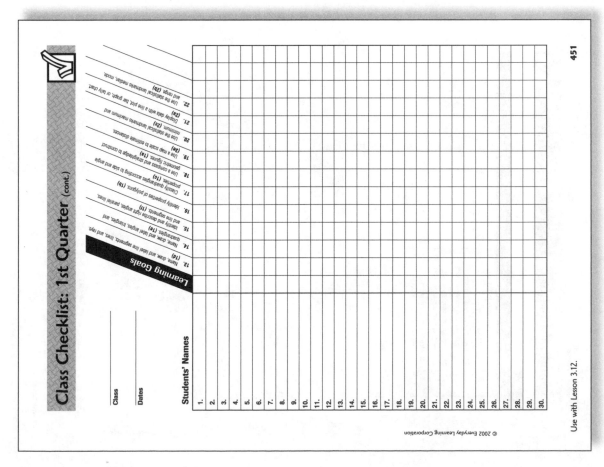

## Individual Profile of Progress: 1st Quarter

Student's Name _____    Date _____

| Check ✓ | | | Learning Goals | Comments |
|---|---|---|---|---|
| B | D | S | | |
| | | | 1. Know addition and subtraction facts. (1g) | |
| | | | 2. Subtract multidigit numbers. (2d) | |
| | | | 3. Add multidigit numbers. (2e) | |
| | | | 4. Read and write numerals to hundred-millions; give the value of the digits in numerals to hundred-millions. (2f) | |
| | | | 5. Find equivalent names for numbers (2g) | |
| | | | 6. Solve open sentences. (3a) | |
| | | | 7. Understand the function and placement of parentheses in number sentences. (3b) | |
| | | | 8. Determine whether number sentences are true or false. (3c) | |
| | | | 9. Solve addition and subtraction number stories. (3d) | |
| | | | 10. Know division facts. (3f) | |
| | | | 11. Know multiplication facts. (3g) | |
| | | | 12. Understand the relationship between multiplication and division. (3h) | |
| | | | 13. Name, draw, and label line segments, lines, and rays. (1d) | |
| | | | 14. Name, draw, and label angles, triangles, and quadrangles. (1e) | |
| | | | 15. Identify and describe right angles, parallel lines, and line segments. (1f) | |
| | | | 16. Identify properties of polygons. (1b) | |
| | | | 17. Classify quadrangles according to side and angle properties. (1c) | |
| | | | 18. Use a compass and straightedge to construct geometric figures. (1a) | |

B = **B**eginning; D = **D**eveloping; S = **S**ecure

452

Use with Lesson 3.12.

## Class Checklist: 1st Quarter (cont.)

Class _____

Dates _____

**Students' Names**

**Learning Goals**

13. Name, draw, and label line segments, lines, and rays. (1d)
14. Name, draw, and label line angles, triangles, and quadrangles. (1e)
15. Identify and describe right angles, triangles, and quadrangles. (1e)
16. Identify properties of polygons. (1b)
17. Classify quadrangles according to side and angle properties. (1c)
18. Use a compass and straightedge to construct geometric figures. (1a)
19. Use a map scale to estimate distances. (3e)
20. Use the statistical landmarks maximum and minimum. (2c)
21. Display data with a line plot, bar graph, or tally chart. (2a)
22. Use the statistical landmarks median, mode, and range (2b)

1. 2. 3. 4. 5. 6. 7. 8. 9. 10. 11. 12. 13. 14. 15. 16. 17. 18. 19. 20. 21. 22. 23. 24. 25. 26. 27. 28. 29. 30.

451

Use with Lesson 3.12.

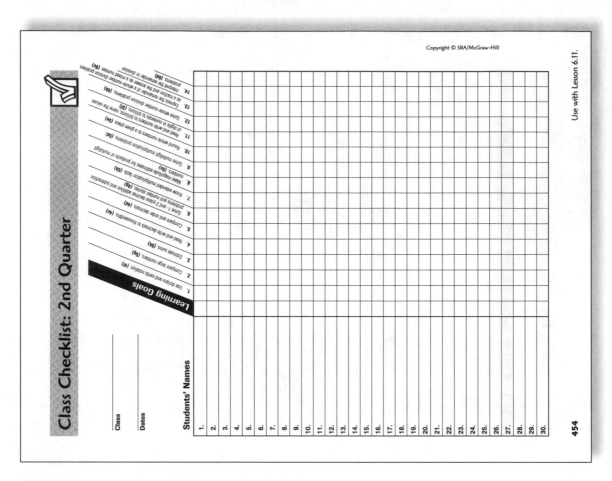

## Class Checklist: 2nd Quarter

Class _____

Dates _____

**Learning Goals**

1. Use dollars-and-cents notation. (4i)
2. Compare large numbers. (5g)
3. Estimate sums. (5h)
4. Read and write decimals to thousandths. (4c)
5. Compare and order decimals. (4d)
6. Solve 1- and 2-place decimal addition and subtraction problems and number stories. (4g)
7. Know extended multiplication facts. (5b)
8. Make magnitude estimates for products of multidigit numbers. (5c)
9. Solve multidigit multiplication problems. (5d)
10. Round whole numbers to a given place. (5e)
11. Read and write numbers to billions; name the values of digits in numerals to billions. (5f)
12. Solve whole-number division problems. (6f)
13. Express the remainder of a whole-number division problem as a fraction and the answer as a mixed number. (6g)
14. Interpret the remainder in division problems. (6d)

**Students' Names**

1.
2.
3.
4.
5.
6.
7.
8.
9.
10.
11.
12.
13.
14.
15.
16.
17.
18.
19.
20.
21.
22.
23.
24.
25.
26.
27.
28.
29.
30.

Use with Lesson 6.11.

454

---

Student's Name _____   Date _____

## Individual Profile of Progress: 1st Quarter

| Check ✓ | | | Learning Goals | Comments |
|---|---|---|---|---|
| B | D | S | | |
| | | | 19. Use a map scale to estimate distances. (3e) | |
| | | | 20. Use the statistical landmarks maximum and minimum. (2c) | |
| | | | 21. Display data with a line plot, bar graph, or tally chart. (2a) | |
| | | | 22. Use the statistical landmarks median, mode, and range. (2b) | |

**Notes to Parents**

**B** = Beginning; **D** = Developing; **S** = Secure

Use with Lesson 3.12.

453

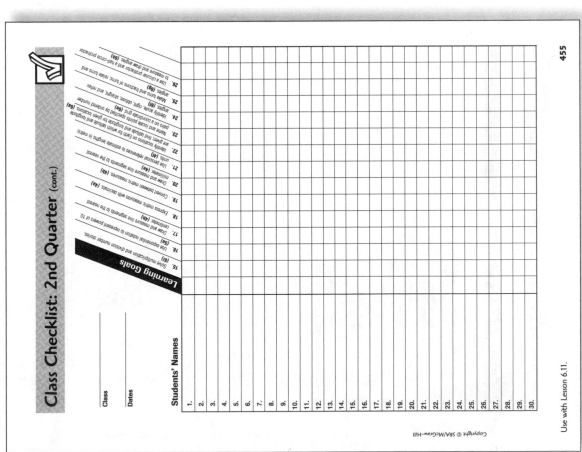

## Individual Profile of Progress: 2nd Quarter

Student's Name _____   Date _____

| Check ✓ | | | Learning Goals | Comments |
|---|---|---|---|---|
| B | D | S | | |
| | | | 1. Use dollars-and-cents notation. (4i) | |
| | | | 2. Compare large numbers. (5g) | |
| | | | 3. Estimate sums. (5h) | |
| | | | 4. Read and write decimals to thousandths. (4c) | |
| | | | 5. Compare and order decimals. (4d) | |
| | | | 6. Solve 1- and 2-place decimal addition and subtraction problems and number stories. (4g) | |
| | | | 7. Know extended multiplication facts. (5b) | |
| | | | 8. Make magnitude estimates for products of multidigit numbers. (5c) | |
| | | | 9. Solve multidigit multiplication problems. (5d) | |
| | | | 10. Round whole numbers to a given place. (5e) | |
| | | | 11. Read and write numbers to billions; name the values of digits in numerals to billions. (5f) | |
| | | | 12. Solve whole-number division problems. (6b) | |
| | | | 13. Express the remainder of a whole-number division problem as a fraction and the answer as a mixed number. (6c) | |
| | | | 14. Interpret the remainder in division problems. (6d) | |
| | | | 15. Solve multiplication and division number stories. (6i) | |
| | | | 16. Use exponential notation to represent powers of 10. (5a) | |
| | | | 17. Draw and measure line segments to the nearest centimeter. (4h) | |
| | | | 18. Express metric measures with decimals. (4a) | |

B = Beginning; D = Developing; S = Secure

456

Use with Lesson 6.11.

## Class Checklist: 2nd Quarter (cont.)

Class _____

Dates _____

**Learning Goals**

15. Solve multiplication and division number stories. (6i)
16. Use exponential notation to represent powers of 10. (5a)
17. Draw and measure line segments to the nearest centimeter. (4h)
18. Express metric measures with decimals. (4a)
19. Convert between metric measures. (4b)
20. Draw and measure line segments to the nearest millimeter. (4e)
21. Use personal references to estimate lengths in metric units. (4f)
22. Identify locations on Earth for which latitude and longitude are given. (6f)
23. Name and locate points specified by ordered number pairs on a coordinate grid. (6e)
24. Identify acute, right, obtuse, straight, and reflex angles. (6h)
25. Make turns and fractions of turns; relate turns and angles. (6g)
26. Use a circular protractor and a half-circle protractor to measure and draw angles. (6a)

**Students' Names**

1.
2.
3.
4.
5.
6.
7.
8.
9.
10.
11.
12.
13.
14.
15.
16.
17.
18.
19.
20.
21.
22.
23.
24.
25.
26.
27.
28.
29.
30.

455

Use with Lesson 6.11.

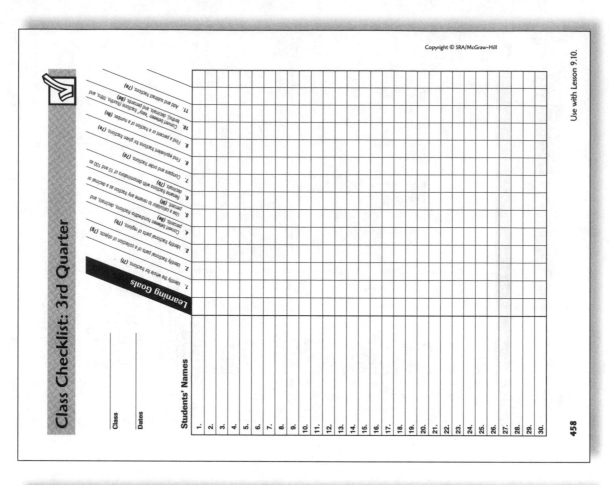

## Class Checklist: 3rd Quarter

Class

Dates

**Learning Goals**

1. Identify the whole for fractions. (7h)
2. Identify fractional parts of a collection of objects. (7g)
3. Identify fractional parts of regions. (7a)
4. Convert between hundredths-fractions, decimals, and percents. (9e)
5. Use a calculator to rename any fraction as a decimal or percent. (9f)
6. Rename fractions with denominators of 10 and 100 as decimals. (7b)
7. Compare and order fractions. (7d)
8. Find equivalent fractions for given fractions. (7c)
9. Find a percent or a fraction of a number. (9c)
10. Convert between "easy" fractions (fourths, fifths, and tenths), decimals, and percents. (9d)
11. Add and subtract fractions. (7e)

**Students' Names**

1.
2.
3.
4.
5.
6.
7.
8.
9.
10.
11.
12.
13.
14.
15.
16.
17.
18.
19.
20.
21.
22.
23.
24.
25.
26.
27.
28.
29.
30.

Use with Lesson 9.10.

458

---

Student's Name

Date

## Individual Profile of Progress: 2nd Quarter

**Check ✓**

| B | D | S | Learning Goals | Comments |
|---|---|---|---|---|
| | | | 19. Convert between metric measures. (4b) | |
| | | | 20. Draw and measure line segments to the nearest millimeter. (4e) | |
| | | | 21. Use personal references to estimate lengths in metric units. (4f) | |
| | | | 22. Identify locations on Earth for which latitude and longitude are given; find latitude and longitude for given locations. (6a) | |
| | | | 23. Name and locate points specified by ordered number pairs on a coordinate grid. (6e) | |
| | | | 24. Identify acute, right, obtuse, straight, and reflex angles. (6f) | |
| | | | 25. Make turns and fractions of turns; relate turns and angles. (6g) | |
| | | | 26. Use a circular protractor and a half-circle protractor to measure and draw angles. (6h) | |

**Notes to Parents**

B = Beginning; D = Developing; S = Secure

Use with Lesson 6.11.

457

---

## Individual Profile of Progress: 3rd Quarter

Student's Name _____  Date _____

| Check ✔ | | | Learning Goals | Comments |
|---|---|---|---|---|
| B | D | S | | |
| | | | 1. Identify the whole for fractions. (7f) | |
| | | | 2. Identify fractional parts of a collection of objects. (7g) | |
| | | | 3. Identify fractional parts of regions. (7h) | |
| | | | 4. Convert between hundredths-fractions, decimals, and percents. (9e) | |
| | | | 5. Use a calculator to rename any fraction as a decimal or percent. (9f) | |
| | | | 6. Rename fractions with denominators of 10 and 100 as decimals. (7b) | |
| | | | 7. Compare and order fractions. (7d) | |
| | | | 8. Find equivalent fractions for given fractions. (7e) | |
| | | | 9. Find a percent or a fraction of a number. (9c) | |
| | | | 10. Convert between "easy" fractions (fourths, fifths, and tenths), decimals, and percents. (9d) | |
| | | | 11. Add and subtract fractions. (7a) | |
| | | | 12. Use an estimation strategy to divide decimals by whole numbers. (9a) | |
| | | | 13. Use an estimation strategy to multiply decimals by whole numbers. (9b) | |
| | | | 14. Apply basic vocabulary and concepts associated with chance events. (7c) | |
| | | | 15. Use formulas to find areas of rectangles, parallelograms, and triangles. (8b) | |
| | | | 16. Find the perimeter of a polygon. (8c) | |
| | | | 17. Find the area of a figure by counting unit squares and fractions of unit squares inside the figure. (8d) | |
| | | | 18. Make and interpret scale drawings. (8a) | |

B = Beginning; D = Developing; S = Secure

460

Use with Lesson 9.10.

---

## Class Checklist: 3rd Quarter (cont.)

Class _____

Dates _____

**Learning Goals**

12. Use an estimation strategy to divide decimals by whole numbers. (9a)
13. Use an estimation strategy to multiply decimals by whole numbers. (9b)
14. Apply basic vocabulary and concepts associated with chance events. (7c)
15. Use formulas to find areas of rectangles, parallelograms, and triangles. (8b)
16. Find the perimeter of a polygon. (8c)
17. Find the area of a figure by counting unit squares and fractions of unit squares inside the figure. (8d)
18. Make and interpret scale drawings. (8a)

**Students' Names**

1.
2.
3.
4.
5.
6.
7.
8.
9.
10.
11.
12.
13.
14.
15.
16.
17.
18.
19.
20.
21.
22.
23.
24.
25.
26.
27.
28.
29.
30.

459

Use with Lesson 9.10.

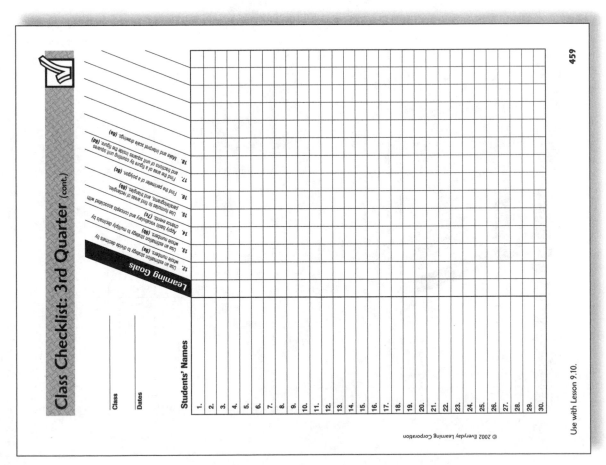

# Class Checklist: 4th Quarter (cont.)

Class _____

Dates _____

**Learning Goals**

12. Rotate figures. (10a)
13. Estimate the weight of objects in ounces or grams; weigh objects in ounces or grams. (11d)
14. Solve cube-stacking volume problems. (11e)
15. Use a formula to calculate volumes of rectangular prisms. (11a)

**Students' Names**

1.
2.
3.
4.
5.
6.
7.
8.
9.
10.
11.
12.
13.
14.
15.
16.
17.
18.
19.
20.
21.
22.
23.
24.
25.
26.
27.
28.
29.
30.

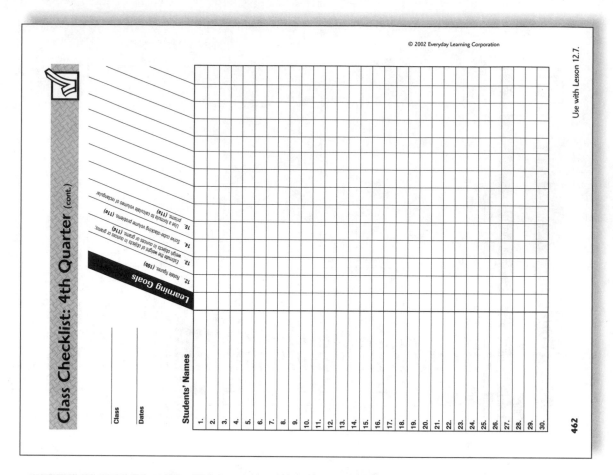

Use with Lesson 12.7.

462

# Class Checklist: 4th Quarter

Class _____

Dates _____

**Learning Goals**

1. Add positive and negative integers. (10a and 11c)
2. Subtract positive and negative integers. (11c)
3. Use rate tables, if necessary, to solve rate problems. (11b)(12a)
4. Find unit rates. (12a)
5. Calculate unit prices to determine which product is the "better buy." (12b)
6. Evaluate reasonableness of rate data. (12c)
7. Collect and compare rate data. (12c)
8. Use a transparent mirror to draw the reflection of a figure. (10d)
9. Identify lines of symmetry, lines of reflection, reflected figures, and figures with line symmetry. (10d)
10. Translate figures. (10a)
11. Describe properties of geometric solids. (11f)

**Students' Names**

1.
2.
3.
4.
5.
6.
7.
8.
9.
10.
11.
12.
13.
14.
15.
16.
17.
18.
19.
20.
21.
22.
23.
24.
25.
26.
27.
28.
29.
30.

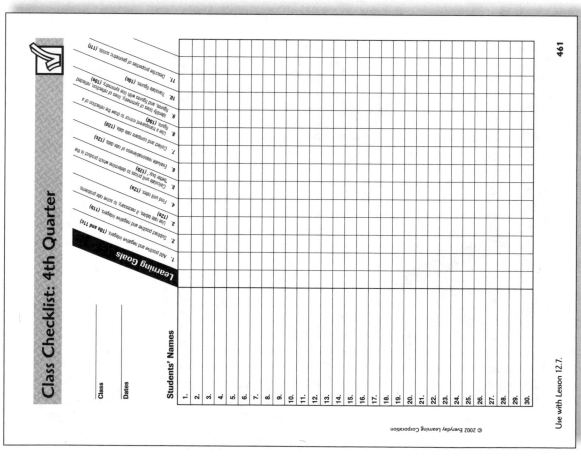

461

Use with Lesson 12.7.

## List of Assessment Sources

**Ongoing Assessment**

**Product Assessment**

**Periodic Assessment**

**Outside Tests**

**Other**

Use as needed.

464

---

Student's Name _____   Date _____

## Individual Profile of Progress: 4th Quarter

| Check ✔ | | | Learning Goals | Comments |
|---|---|---|---|---|
| B | D | S | | |
| | | | 1. Add positive and negative integers. **(10a and 11c)** | |
| | | | 2. Subtract positive and negative integers. **(11b)** | |
| | | | 3. Use rate tables, if necessary, to solve rate problems. **(12e)** | |
| | | | 4. Find unit rates. **(12a)** | |
| | | | 5. Calculate unit prices to determine which product is the "better buy." **(12b)** | |
| | | | 6. Evaluate reasonableness of rate data. **(12c)** | |
| | | | 7. Collect and compare rate data. **(12d)** | |
| | | | 8. Use a transparent mirror to draw the reflection of a figure. **(10d)** | |
| | | | 9. Identify lines of symmetry, lines of reflection, reflected figures, and figures with line symmetry. **(10e)** | |
| | | | 10. Translate figures. **(10c)** | |
| | | | 11. Describe properties of geometric solids. **(11f)** | |
| | | | 12. Rotate figures. **(10b)** | |
| | | | 13. Estimate the weight of objects in ounces or grams; weigh objects in ounces or grams. **(11d)** | |
| | | | 14. Solve cube-stacking volume problems. **(11e)** | |
| | | | 15. Use a formula to calculate volumes of rectangular prisms. **(11a)** | |

**Notes to Parents**

B = Beginning; D = Developing; S = Secure

Use with Lesson 12.7.

463

## Class Checklist

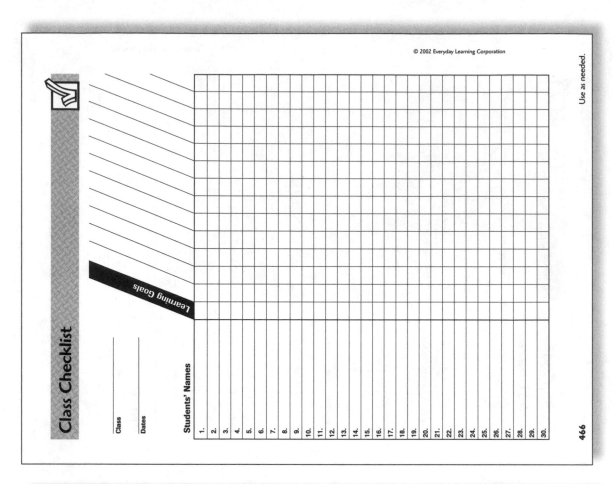

Class _____

Dates _____

Learning Goals

**Students' Names**

1.
2.
3.
4.
5.
6.
7.
8.
9.
10.
11.
12.
13.
14.
15.
16.
17.
18.
19.
20.
21.
22.
23.
24.
25.
26.
27.
28.
29.
30.

Use as needed.

466

---

Student's Name _____ Date _____

## Individual Profile of Progress

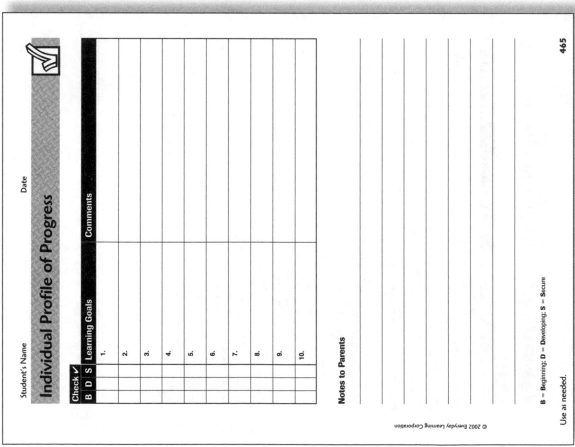

| Check ✔ | | | Learning Goals | Comments |
|---|---|---|---|---|
| B | D | S | | |
| | | | 1. | |
| | | | 2. | |
| | | | 3. | |
| | | | 4. | |
| | | | 5. | |
| | | | 6. | |
| | | | 7. | |
| | | | 8. | |
| | | | 9. | |
| | | | 10. | |

**Notes to Parents**

B = Beginning; **D** = Developing; **S** = Secure

Use as needed.

465

## Evaluating My Math Class

Name _____  Date _____

© 2002 Everyday Learning Corporation

### Interest Inventory

| Dislike a Lot 1 | Dislike 2 | Neither Like nor Dislike 3 | Like 4 | Like a Lot 5 |
|---|---|---|---|---|

Use the scale above to describe how you feel about:

1. your math class.  _____

2. working with a partner or in a group.  _____

3. working by yourself.  _____

4. solving problems.  _____

5. making up problems for others to solve.  _____

6. finding new ways to solve problems.  _____

7. challenges in math class.  _____

8. playing mathematical games.  _____

9. working on Study Links.  _____

10. working on projects that take more than a day to complete.  _____

11. Which math lesson has been your favorite so far? Why?

_____

_____

_____

_____

_____

_____

Use as needed.

468

---

## Class Progress Indicator

Mathematical Topic Being Assessed: _____

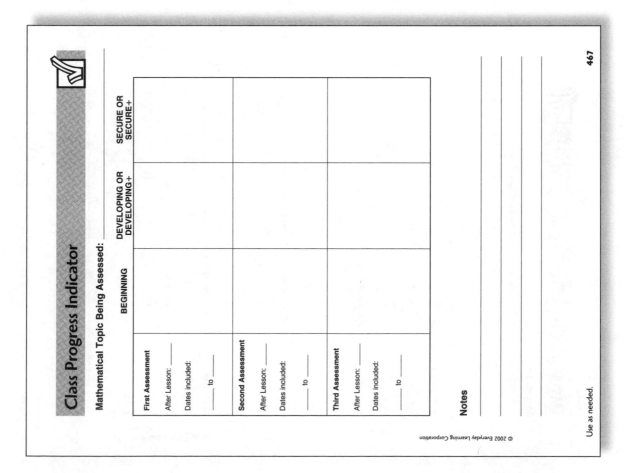

| | BEGINNING | DEVELOPING OR DEVELOPING+ | SECURE OR SECURE+ |
|---|---|---|---|
| **First Assessment** <br> After Lesson: ___ <br> Dates included: ___ to ___ | | | |
| **Second Assessment** <br> After Lesson: ___ <br> Dates included: ___ to ___ | | | |
| **Third Assessment** <br> After Lesson: ___ <br> Dates included: ___ to ___ | | | |

**Notes** _____

_____

_____

Use as needed.

© 2002 Everyday Learning Corporation

467

## Weekly Math Log

Name _____ Date _____

**1.** What did you study in math this week?

_____
_____
_____
_____
_____

**2.** Many ideas in math are related to other ideas within math. Think about how the topic(s) you studied in class this week relate to other topics you learned before.

Your reflection can include what you learned in previous years.

_____
_____
_____
_____
_____
_____

Use as needed.

**470**

## My Math Class

Name _____ Date _____

**Interest Inventory**

**1.** In math class, I am good at _____
_____

**2.** One thing I like about math is _____
_____

**3.** One thing I find difficult in mathematics class is _____
_____

**4.** The most interesting thing I have learned in math so far this year is _____
_____

**5.** Outside school, I used mathematics when I _____
_____

**6.** I would like to know more about _____
_____

Use as needed.

**469**

Name _____  Date _____

## Number-Story Math Log

1. Write an easy number story that uses mathematical ideas that you have studied recently. Solve the problem.

**Number Story** _____

**Solution** _____

2. Write a difficult number story that uses mathematical ideas that you have studied recently. If you can, solve the number story. If you are not able to solve it, explain what you need to know to solve it.

**Number Story** _____

**Solution** _____

Use as needed.

472

---

Name _____  Date _____

## Math Log

Use as needed.

471

Name _____ Date _____

## Sample Math Work

**Self-Assessment**

Attach a sample of your work to this form.

**1.** This work is an example of:

_____
_____
_____

**2.** This work shows that I can:

_____
_____

**OPTIONAL**

**3.** This work shows that I still need to improve:

_____
_____
_____

Use as needed.

**473**

---

Name _____ Date _____

## Discussion of My Math Work

**Self-Assessment**

Attach a sample of your work to this page. Tell what you think is important about your sample.

_____
_____
_____
_____
_____
_____

Use as needed.

**474**

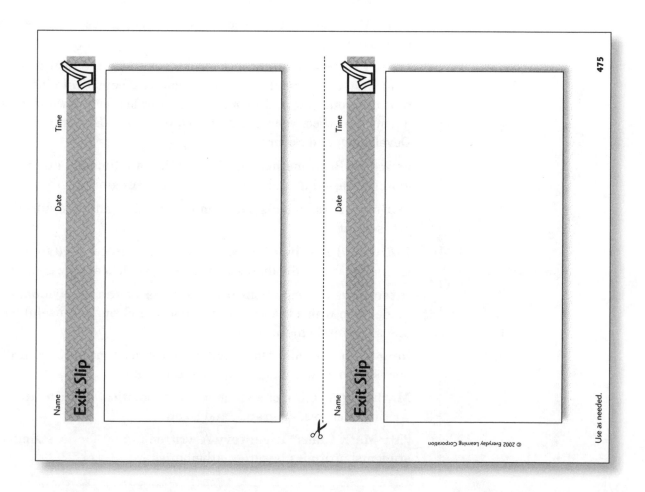

Name _____

**Exit Slip**

Date _____

Time _____

Name _____

**Exit Slip**

Date _____

Time _____

Use as needed.

© 2002 Everyday Learning Corporation

475

# Glossary

**anecdotal records** Brief, pertinent pieces of information gathered during informal observation.

**assessment** The gathering of information about students' progress. This might include their knowledge and use of mathematics, as well as their feelings about their mathematical progress. This information is used to draw conclusions for individual and class instruction.

**assessment plan** A balanced group of assessment activities chosen by an individual teacher.

**assessment sources** Mathematical tasks or interactions that can be used for gathering data for assessment purposes.

**Class Checklist** A tool used to record ongoing observations and interactions.

**Class Progress Indicator** A form upon which the results of sequential assessment tasks for various mathematical ideas, routines, concepts, and so on, can be recorded for the whole class during the school year using such categories as Beginning, Developing, and Secure.

**concepts** Basic mathematical ideas that are fundamental in guiding reasoning and problem solving in unfamiliar situations.

**evaluation** Judgments based on information gathered during assessment.

**Individual Profile of Progress** A recording tool used to measure the progress of individual students on specific learning goals.

**interviews** Conversations between a teacher and individual students in which the teacher can obtain information useful for assessing mathematical progress.

**long-term projects** Mathematical activities that may require time spans of days, weeks, or months to complete.

**Math Log** A record of a student's mathematical thinking through writing, pictures, diagrams, and so on.

**"My Math Class" Inventory** A written format for assessing students' attitudes toward mathematics.

**observation** Watching and recording students' interactions and communications during regular instructional activities.

**Ongoing Assessment** The gathering of assessment data during regular instructional activities, mostly through observation.

**open-ended questions** Questions that have multiple answers and strategies for arriving at the answers. (Open-ended questions are good assessments for problem solving and reasoning.)

**Outside Tests** Usually tests at the school, district, or state level, or nationally standardized tests. If these tests do not match the curriculum, they may not provide valid assessment information.

**performance** The carrying out or completing of a mathematical activity that displays a student's knowledge and judgment while he or she is engaged in the activity.

**Periodic Assessment** The more formal gathering of assessment information, often outside of regular instructional time. One example is end-of-unit assessments.

**Portfolio** A sample collection of a student's mathematical work and related writing representing his or her progress over the school year.

**Product Assessment** Samples of students' work, which may include pictures, diagrams, or concrete representations.

**progress** The growth, development, and continuous improvement of students' mathematical abilities.

**Progress Indicator** See Class Progress Indicator.

**reflective writing** The ability to reflect and write about mathematics as it relates to accomplishments, confidence, feelings, understanding or lack of understanding, goals, and so on.

**representative work** A piece of work that represents students' ability and reflects students' progress.

**rubric** A set of guidelines for scoring assessment activities. The most useful rubrics are those derived from experience with a wide variety of performances on an assessment task.

**self-assessment** The ability of students to judge, reflect on, acknowledge, and improve the quality of their mathematical thinking or productions.

**standardized tests** Typically, nationwide tests that are given, scored, and interpreted in a very consistent way, regardless of the population being tested.

**strategies** The thoughts and procedures an individual student uses to solve a problem.

**validity of assessment** The degree to which assessment data actually represent the knowledge, thought processes, and skills that students have attained.

# Index